in Italian

The all-in-one language and travel guide

Rossella Peressini
Robert Andrews

BBC Books

Developed by BBC Languages
Series advisor: Derek Utley
Edited by Tracy Miller
Audio producer: John Green, tefl tapes
Concept design by Carroll Associates
Typeset and designed by Book Creation Services, London

Cover design by Carroll Associates
Cover photo: Pictor International, London
Map: Malcolm Porter

ISBN 0 563 40054 4

Published by BBC Books, a division of BBC Worldwide Ltd
First published 1998
Reprinted 2000, 2002(Twice)
Printed and bound in Great Britain by Ebenezer Baylis & Son Ltd, Worcester
Colour seperations by DOT Gradations, England

Photographs
All photographs by Ian Howes, except:

Pictor International p4(b), 7(t), 8, 18(t), 21, 22(tl), 23
Getty Images p9, 10, 15(b), 19, 20(t), 22(tr,b), 35(b), 46(m,b), 53, 91(b)
Zefa Pictures p15(t), 16(b)
Cephas p16(t), 24(t), 77(t), 80, 85(tl), 86, 87
Life File p18(b), 20(b), 36(t), 48(l), 49, 50(r), 51, 52
Anthony Blake p47(b), 81, 82, 83, 84(tr,bl,br), 85, 89
Allsport International p90(tl,m)

Due to the scale of the map, it has not been possible to include full
details; however, every care has been taken to include as many of the
places mentioned in the book as possible.

Every care has been taken to ensure that all facts contained in this book
were correct at time of publication.

INTRODUCTION

Get By in Italian will enable you to pick up the language, travel with confidence and experience the very best the country has to offer. You can use it both *before* a trip, to pick up the basics of the language and to plan your itinerary, and *during* your trip, as a phrasebook and as a source of practical information in all the key travel situations.

Contents
Insider's guide to Italy An introduction to the country, a guide to the main cities and region-by-region highlights for planning itineraries

Bare necessities The absolute essentials of Italian

Seven main chapters covering key travel situations from *Getting around* to *Entertainment and leisure*. Each chapter has three main sections: *information* to help you understand the local way of doing things; *Phrasemaker*, a phrasebook of key words and phrases; *Language works / Try it out*, simple dialogues and activities to help you remember the language.

Menu reader A key to menus in Italian

Language builder A simple introduction to Italian grammar

1000-word dictionary The most important Italian words you will come across with their English translations.

Sounds Italian A clear guide to pronouncing the language

How to use the book
Before you go You can use the *Insider's guide* to get a flavour of the country and plan where you want to go. To pick up the language, the *Phrasemaker* sections give you the key words and phrases; the *Language works* dialogues show the language in action, and *Try it out* offers you a chance to practise for yourself.

During your trip The *Insider's guide* offers tips on the best things to see and do in the main cities. The *Phrasemaker* works as a phrasebook with all the key language to help you get what you want. Within each chapter there is also practical 'survival' information to help you get around and understand the country.

Insider's guide to Italy

Perugia

Italy's historical setting

Although only a nation since the last century, Italy has been at the centre of European culture for two millennia. Its capital of Rome was the heart of a vast military empire, and, following that empire's demise, became the seat of the Catholic church. In the Middle Ages the growth of independent city-states, such as Venice, Florence, Pisa and Genoa, gave rise to a patronage of the arts which found its full flowering in the Renaissance.

While Italy's rich artistic and intellectual traditions exerted a powerful influence on Western culture, politically it was diffuse and weak. This situation prevailed until the nineteenth century, when the nationalist movement under Garibaldi, Cavour and others led to the creation of the kingdom of Italy in 1861, with complete unification ten years later.

In the 20th century, a new democratic republic grew from the ashes of Fascist government and the Second World War. Despite chronic political uncertainty at national level, Italy has become one of Europe's most advanced technological nations, though there remain acute inequalities between the rich, industrialized North and the more rural economy of the depressed South. The enduring artistic monuments, the strong gastronomic tradition and the dramatic beauty of its landscape have made Italy one of the most visited countries in the world.

The Italian people

The famously passionate and gregarious nature of the Italians has much to do with the largely congenial Mediterranean climate which encourages an open, outdoor society. There are strong regional differences which are the legacy of quite separate political and cultural traditions, and are still reflected today in distinct dialects, often incomprehensible to most Italians let alone foreigners. On the whole, however, the stereotype of a voluble, style-conscious and life-loving people holds true throughout the country.

The influence of the Catholic Church, though diminished, is strong throughout Italy, closely linked to the central role of the family. The Italian psyche is characterized by impatience and long-suffering endurance, by a deep cynicism and an ardent warmth, and by a generosity of spirit and an unashamed sentimentality, particularly concerning children.

Italy's geography and climate

The north of Italy, from the Alps to Rome, comprises a wide range of landscapes. The coasts are amongst the most scenic in Europe, and one can find both popular resorts (such as those on the Italian Riviera and, on the east, Rimini) and unspoiled beaches. The climate on the coasts is hot and dry in summer and mild in winter, though the sea will be too cold for most people between October and May. In the Alps and the Apennines in winter, heavy snowfalls can close roads and delay trains. There is good skiing December to March, and autumn and spring are the best seasons for hill-walking. Between the Alps and the Apennines the extensive plains of the Po valley hold some of the most attractive cities of northern Italy, including Bologna, Parma, Ferrara and Ravenna. Here, the climate is characterized by grey skies and mists in winter and suffocating heat in summer: August and January/February are best avoided. Further down, Tuscany and Umbria are predominantly hilly. Here and in Rome, high summer can be too hot for sightseeing, and while August in the cities can be relatively quiet, it

would be a pity to miss out on city life in full swing. The spring is more conducive to sightseeing and has a unique quality of light, while the shifting hues of the countryside in autumn make a good argument for a visit between September and December.

As a rule, the further south you go, the warmer it is, though the mountains in Campania and Calabria offer cooler temperatures. The main attractions, however, are the islands, coastal resorts and archaeological sites, for which spring offers the clearest light and bluest skies. Naples is the major urban centre (and best avoided altogether in the hectic summer months). The élite islands of Capri and Ischia in the Bay of Naples also become congested in July and August, as do the towns and coastal roads of the Amalfi coast. Puglia, which is predominantly flat, is easy to tour even in winter.

Again, spring and autumn are the best seasons to visit Sicily. July and August see the densest crowds on the coasts and in the main tourist centres. Swimming is best between June and September, with the water

Venice

can still find areas of remote, sandy beaches. For greater isolation, however, many prefer to escape to the islands, such as the far-flung Aeolians, off the northern coast. Taormina and Cefalù are popular at all times, with the package-tours most intense during Easter, Christmas and high summer. Palermo and Siracusa are good bases for cultural excursions to such places as Agrigento (Greek ruins) and Piazza Armerina (Roman mosaics).

at its warmest towards the end of summer. Although much of Sicily's seaboard has been built over, you

Currency/Changing money

The cost of living varies greatly between north and south: the south is relatively cheap and only now starting to exploit its tourist potential, while the north is quite expensive. Most hotels, restaurants, petrol stations and larger stores accept credit cards; cheques are less common, and not accepted in petrol stations. Most banks will change cash and traveller's cheques, and an increasing number will take credit cards. Automatic cash machines can be found in the tourist centres. Banks open Monday to Friday 9 am–1 pm and for an hour around 3–4 in the afternoon (these times vary locally). Some travel agencies and hotels can change money, and larger towns have independent exchanges which stay open later, especially around railway stations. Major tourist centres also have automatic machines which change foreign currency.

Visas and entry requirements

St Peter's, Rome

All visitors to Italy need to present a full passport.

Citizens of the European Union do not need a visa and may stay for up to 90 days before needing to apply for a permit at the local *Questura* (police headquarters). Visitors from the United States, Canada, South Africa, Australia or New Zealand do not need a visa if staying for less than three months. For addresses of embassies and consulates in Italy, see p100.

Rome

*R*ome has probably inspired more eulogies in poetry, film and song than any other city. It is a fast, exciting place, while still retaining its ancient glamour, and owes much of its sensuous appeal to this vibrant frisson between the old and new. You never need to walk far to have your breath taken away by a stirring vista or a sight of rare beauty, often a survival from one of the diverse eras whose relics jostle for attention. Although it is Italy's capital, Rome has much smaller, more manageable dimensions than, say, Milan, and a very distinct character.

Don't miss

An ice-cream on the Spanish Steps, after window-shopping in the elegant boutiques around Via del Corso.

A stroll through Villa Borghese, a lovely park providing welcome respite from summer heat; from the Pincio hill there are stupendous views over the rooftops of Rome.

The Vatican Museums, one of the world's greatest repositories of art; all tours should take in Michelangelo's newly-restored frescos in the Sistine Chapel.

St Peter's, the heart of Catholic culture and always thronged with an international crowd of worshippers and sightseers.

Porta Portese, a Sunday-morning flea market between the Tiber and Viale Trastevere, good for clothes and curios; arrive early.

The Colosseum, the immemorial symbol of Rome's ancient grandeur, next to the Arch of Constantine at one end of the Forum.

A refresher in Campo de' Fiori, fruit and flower market by day, meeting-point by night, with cafés and restaurants on the square, and a web of boutique-lined lanes round about.

The Protestant Cemetery, worth the excursion to the old city walls, where the poets Keats and Shelley are interred.

The Pantheon, the best-preserved of the old Roman remains, thanks to its transformation into a church and subsequently a shrine: Michelangelo and the kings of Italy are buried here.

A Sunday-morning wander through Trastevere, followed by a climb up the Janiculum Hill to enjoy Rome's greatest vista.

Colosseum

Clubs and bars

Alien (Via Velletri) Thoroughly modern, attracting a well-heeled crowd. Art events during the day.
Alexanderplatz (Via Ostia) Features jazz and blues concerts. There is a restaurant too.
Sant'Eustachio (Piazza Sant' Eustachio) Renowned for its frothy cappuccinos and strong espressos.
Castello (Via di Porta Castello) Often queues to get in, but worth the wait.
Piper 90 (Via Tagliamento) Established, if passé. Reliable mix of dance music from all eras.
Gilda (Via Mario de' Fiori) Includes bar, nightclub and restaurant, popular with jetsetters and celebrities.
Caffè del Marzio (Piazza Santa Maria in Trastevere) A good stop-off before or after an evening on the town.

Have an ice-cream or pastry in

Bernasconi (Largo Argentina) A busy pastry-shop, famous among the cognoscenti.
Tre Scalini (Piazza Navona) Specializes in the rich, chocolaty *tartufo* ice-cream.
Bar della Pace (Piazza Navona) For those who want a front-row seat to see and be seen.
Giolitti (near the Pantheon) One of Rome's most prestigious ice-cream parlours.
Gelateria della Palma (near Giolitti) Serves a range of adventurously flavoured ice-creams in a high-tech ambience.
Canova Café and Café Rosati (Piazza del Popolo) Two long-established rivals. You can have a full meal at the Canova, which also has a courtyard.
Antico Caffè Greco (Via Condotti) A good stop on any window-shopping tour of Rome's most elegant boutiques.
Caffè de Paris (Via Veneto) Basks in memories of its Dolce Vita heyday, and still draws a posh clientele.
Al Ristoro della Salute (behind the Colosseum) For a cone or drink before tackling Rome's grandest ancient monument.
Pasticceria Cecere (Trastevere) A good place for breakfast or a zabaglione dessert.

Have a meal in

Dal Bolognese (Piazza del Popolo) A fashionable, arty restaurant specializing in cuisine from Bologna. Moderate.
La Carbonara (Campo de' Fiori) Excellent antipasti. Expensive.
Il Convivio (Via dell'Orso, off Piazza Navona) A small establishment offering highly-rated meals. Expensive.
Ivo (Via di San Francesco a Ripa) A Trastevere institution – queues are common for the authentic and low-priced pizzas. Cheap.
Grappolo d'Oro (Piazza della Cancelleria, off Campo de' Fiori). Its reasonably-priced daily specials are popular; there are a few outside tables. Moderate.
Hostaria Farnese (Via dei Baullari, between Campo de' Fiori and Piazza Farnese) A tiny, family-run place with the accent on fresh produce from the market. Moderate.
Al Moro (Vicolo delle Bollete, near the Trevi Fountain) Packed with

atmosphere and charm; frequented by the in-crowd in the 1960s. Moderate.

Otello alla Concordia (Via della Croce, off Piazza di Spagna) Eat indoors or out. Moderate.

Piperno (Monte dei Cenci) In the old Jewish Ghetto, this restaurant exudes an authentic Old World dignity. Expensive.

Pizzeria Remo (Santa Maria Liberatrice, Testaccio) A reliable, no-frills pizzeria. Cheap.

Children's Rome

Rome is not a particularly amenable place for children, with the congestion and pavement-parked cars especially a nightmare for anyone with a push-chair. Villa Borghese is one place where they can run around without risk; you might also try Luna Park, a fairground in the EUR section of the city. Back in town, the Castel Sant'Angelo has plenty to keep children happy.

Rome's transport

Driving in Rome is not to be recommended. Fortunately there is a good system of public transport: tickets can be bought at most *tabacchini* (tobacconist's) or at stations and main terminals.

City buses

The main bus station is right outside Termini railway station. Equip yourself with a route-map from a newsagent or ticket office. As a rule, board at the back and exit from the central doors. Buy tickets in advance and stamp them as soon as you board. Ask about day- and week-tickets.

There is a limited tram service: the 110 is a cheap if slow way to see many of the city's most important sights.

Useful bus routes

Number 46: Piazza Venezia to the Vatican

Number 64: Termini to the Vatican, via Piazza Venezia

Number 170: Termini to Trastevere

Number 119: a minibus on a circular route through the old centre

The Metropolitana

Rome has a limited but useful underground service, with two lines – A and B – which meet at Termini. The service runs from about 5.30 am to midnight, and discounted books of tickets valid for bus and Metropolitana are available.

Useful Metropolitana stops

Piazza di Spagna and Flaminio: Via del Corso, the Spanish Steps, Piazza del Popolo and Villa Borghese

Colosseo: the Colosseum and Forum

Ottaviano: the Vatican

Daytrips from Rome

Ostia Antica

Once Rome's main port, then silted over with a mud that helped to preserve much of the town, Ostia Antica is an extensive archaeological zone. Mosaics, temples, a theatre and the remains of private houses help to recreate town-life as it was in the classical era. Get there by trains on the Ostiense line, accessible from Magliana on Metro Line B.

Villa d'Este, Tivoli

departures from outside the station at Rebibbia, on Metro line B.

Lago di Bracciano

A brief drive or bus-ride north will bring you to this calm water famous for its eels. Sample them in lakeside restaurants in Anguillara or the town of Bracciano, dominated by the Castello Orsini-Odelscalchi.

Frascati

Frascati is the most popular of the Castelli Romani (hill towns). Villa Aldobrandini affords wonderful views back over Rome and you can sample the local *porchetta* (roast pork) sold from stalls. The area is best explored by car, though you can reach Frascati and other Castelli by train from Termini or bus from Cinecittà (on Metro line A).

Anzio and the Pontine Islands

Anzio, a pleasant resort south of Rome, boasts some good fish restaurants, and is an embarkation point for the Pontine Islands.

Tivoli

Combine a trip to the Villa d'Este gardens at Tivoli, with their elaborate fountains, and a visit to the spectacular ruins of Hadrian's Villa. It's an extensive site, so take a picnic. The gardens and the villa are about a kilometre apart, both reachable on a ACOTRAL bus with frequent

Anzio

Florence

The capital of Tuscany, the region which spawned the Italian Renaissance, Florence's magnetic appeal is not merely due to its artistic treasures, piazzas, churches and marvellous vistas, but also to the less visible resonances of its illustrious past. The city is at its best in low season: wander through the San Lorenzo market, savour the piazzas from a well-appointed bar, absorb the church interiors from a quiet pew. You should also leave time for day-excursions to the less-visited, outlying attractions and to sample the stunning Tuscan countryside.

Duomo

Don't miss

The Uffizi gallery, the richest of Florence's art collections, packed with familiar paintings and sculptures.

Museo Nazionale del Bargello, with work by Michelangelo and Donatello, including the latter's remarkable David.

The medieval Ponte Vecchio, most photogenic of the bridges crossing the Arno, and the only one spared by the retreating Nazis in 1944.

Santa Maria del Carmine, for the superbly restored fresco cycle by Masaccio which inspired artists of the rank of Leonardo da Vinci, Michelangelo, Filippino Lippi, Botticelli and Raphael.

The Pitti Palace, Florence's largest Renaissance palace was the home of the ruling Medici family. It now houses a suite of museums with works by Raphael.

The Galleria Accademia, where Michelangelo's David stands, locally known as 'Il Gigante', a powerful symbol of the Florentine Renaissance. Other works by Michelangelo and by other pre-eminent names are also here.

A hot chocolate in winter or an ice-cream in summer, in one of the bars in Piazza della Signoria, for a view of the statuary outside the Palazzo Vecchio.

The Duomo, focal point of Florence, its imposing dome by Brunelleschi helping to create one of the most recognizable profiles of any city. The building forms part of an ensemble along with Giotto's Campanile (bell-tower) and the octagonal Battistero (Baptistery), whose bronze doors by Ghiberti are one of the wonders of the Renaissance.

The Boboli gardens, ranged behind the Pitti Palace in a series of landscaped terraces, ideal for a stroll, picnic and siesta.

Hearing the Gregorian chants in the church of San Miniato al Monte, possibly the most beautiful Romanesque church in Florence.

River Arno

From outside, or from the nearby Piazzale Michelangelo, the views over the city are stupendous, especially at sunset.

Have a drink, ice-cream or meal in

Rivoire (Piazza della Signoria) For a pastry and coffee on Florence's main square. Expensive.

La Maremmana (Via de' Macci, Santa Croce) Serves traditional Tuscan fare at very reasonable prices. Diners sit at long tables and slurp *ribollita*, the local soup made with white beans and bread. Cheap.

Angiolino (Via Santo Spirito, Oltrarno) Has a charcoal grill used to prepare Tuscan specialities. Moderate.

Gilli (Piazza della Repubblica) One of the oldest cafés in Florence.

Gelateria Vivoli (Via Isole delle Stinche, Santa Croce) Still reckoned the best in town for ice-creams – a Florentine institution. Often busy.

Oreste (Piazza Santo Spirito, Oltrarno) You can enjoy Tuscan dishes outside. Moderate.

Giacosa (Via Tornabuoni) Reputed birthplace of the Negroni cocktail; good also for its coffees and pastries.

Cabiria (Piazza Santo Spirito) A bar popular with the younger set, especially at night.

Acqua al Due (Via delle Vigna Vecchia, near the Bargello) A tiny place with a casual atmosphere and a selection of pasta dishes for first course to be shared by everyone at the table. Moderate.

Caffè Strozzi (Piazza Strozzi) A stylish bar with outside tables.

Le Mossacce (Via del Proconsolo, midway between the Duomo and the Bargello) An old artists' haunt now popular with Florentines and tourists alike. Cheap.

Festival del Gelato (Via del Corso) It offers 100 flavours of ice-cream.

Children's Florence

A cultural tour of Florence is not the ideal pastime for children, though there are some things which will appeal. The Boboli Gardens, for example, where such curiosities as the famous sculpture of the court jester riding on a turtle's back are fun, not to mention the ornamental fountains and long grassy slopes. A visit to Florence at the end of June will coincide with the games of Calcio Storico, a version of football organized to arcane, centuries-old rules, with spectacular costumes and fireworks.

Florence's transport

Florence is best negotiated on foot. When necessary, use the ATAF buses, most of which leave from the rail station or Piazza del Duomo.

City buses

Tickets are valid for one or two hours, or for the whole day, and can be bought at the *tabacchi* or ticket machines.

Useful bus routes

Number 7: station to Fiesole via the old centre

Number 12 or 13: station to Piazzale Michelangelo

Number 17B: station to the city youth hostel

Number 23C: airport to the railway station

Siena

Daytrips from Florence

Fiesole The easiest excursion from
Florence is to what is now a hilltop
suburb, formerly an important
Etruscan settlement. The Cattedrale
di San Romolo pales in comparison
with the architectural masterpieces
of Florence, but there is interest in
the bare Romanesque interior.
Concerts take place in the Roman
theatre in the archaeological zone
nearby.

Siena Many people prefer the
smaller-scale Siena to Florence.
Out of season, and best of all early
on a weekday morning, the town
reveals its true charm, a harmonious
ensemble of medieval town-
planning, with not a little art to
admire.

A tour through Chianti country
South of Florence lies the heart of the
Chianti grape-growing area, the
prize vineyards spread over classic
undulating Tuscan countryside.
Head for Greve and Radda in
Chianti, making sure to have a meal
en route.

A drive to San Gimignano One of
the few Tuscan towns to have
preserved at least a proportion of its
medieval towers. Even though only
14 of an estimated 72 remain, the
effect is nonetheless impressive, with
the highest, La Rognosa, reaching
more than 160ft. San Gimignano is
also the home of one of Tuscany's
few white wines, Vernaccia.

Pisa Although access is currently
barred while essential work is done
to counter the increasing tilt, and
there are doubts about future access,
the Leaning Tower of Pisa is an
essential stop. In any case, the real
marvel here is the composite of
architectural grace it forms together
with the Duomo and Baptistery on
the Campo dei Miracoli, or 'Field
of Miracles'.

The Medici Villas The Medici family
ruled Florence for three centuries.
These opulent villas were the fruit of
the massive wealth the family
accumulated during the 15th and
16th centuries. Three of the villas are
conveniently close to one another
and exhibit sumptuous rooms and
spectacular gardens. There are bus
services to most leaving from outside
Florence's railway station.

Outdoor activities in the Mugello
Between Florence and the border
with Emilia-Romagna, the hills of
the Mugello offer ideal terrain for
gentle pony-trekking, while the
Sieve river attracts canoeists.

Venice

*V*enice, one of the great tourist cities of the world, has been in peril for as long as any of us can remember: its very fragility and decay form part of its unique fascination, the city's sorry and waterlogged state all the more poignant when cast against its fabulous past. The dominant maritime power in the Mediterranean for four centuries, the city owes much of its extraordinary character to the influence of the East and Venice's connections with it through trade and later war. The many looted statues and icons throughout the city testify to the republic's military prowess, while its great commercial success is embodied in the sumptuous merchants' palaces which line the Grand Canal and the hoards of art treasures in its museums. The city's cultural wealth justifies an intensive tour of its churches and galleries, but its real allure lies in simply meandering through the streets and piazzas on foot or by water.

Don't miss

An ice-cream or cappuccino in Piazza San Marco, 'the most elegant drawing room in Europe'. Probably the most expensive too, but worth the splurge.

Recalling scenes from the film *Death in Venice,* at the Lido, a place to lounge, pose or promenade (but not to swim, given the murky water).

A trip to the islands in the Lagoon, Burano and Torcello Burano is famed for its lace-making, on show at the lace museum, while Torcello's 7th-century church of Santa Maria Assunta was Venice's first cathedral: it has splendid mosaics.

The Peggy Guggenheim Collection, housed in an unfinished 18th-century palazzo on the Grand Canal, where the American heiress lived; it features Rothko, Pollock, Chagall and Picasso, among other modern masters.

St Mark's Basilica, the prime sight in Piazza San Marco, and quite unlike any other cathedral in the world.

A gondola ride OK, it's a cliché, and an expensive one at that, but gondolas are really the ultimate Venetian experience; second-best, and more affordable, is a ride on a *vaporetto* (water bus): service no. 1 traces the whole course of the Grand Canal.

The Rialto market, a lively fruit and vegetable market, but once the core of the city's commercial life, where goods from throughout the Orient were traded. After a stroll here, pause on the Rialto bridge, for the view of the Grand Canal and the Gothic *palazzi* that line it.

The glass museums World-famous glass is manufactured and sold on the island of Murano.

The Accademia, the most important gallery in Venice, spanning 500 years of the city's artistic achievements, from the Byzantine-influenced 14th century to the High Renaissance and beyond. Most absorbing are the scenes of Venice itself.

The Campanile in Piazza San Marco, the tallest structure in Venice – climb and admire the city's stupendous skyline.

The Palazzo Ducale, the old Doges' Palace, already 500 years old before it was revamped in the Gothic style in the 14th and 15th centuries. Visit the dank and menacing prisons, reachable from the Palazzo across the famous Bridge of Sighs.

Have a drink, ice-cream or meal in

Florian and Quadri (Piazza San Marco) The two oldest bars in Venice: both are opulently furnished and have mini-orchestras to create a real period atmosphere. Expensive.

Vino Vino (Calle delle Veste, near Campo San Fantin) A wine bar which also serves sandwiches and quick meals. Very busy. Cheap.

Da Fiore (Calle del Scaleter off Campo San Polo) The place to eat seafood – reservations essential Expensive.

Gelateria Paolin (Campo Santo Stefano) A wide range of ice-creams. Very busy.

Da Gianni (Fondamenta Zátere) Meals can be enjoyed outdoors overlooking the Canale della Giudecca. Moderate.

Pasticceria Marchini (Calle del Spezier, off Campo Santo Stefano) Superlative pastries made to centuries-old recipes.

Harry's Bar (Calle Vallaresso, behind Piazza San Marco) The prototype of a host of imitators around the world. *The* place to be seen with a cocktail. You can also have sandwiches or full-blown meals here. Expensive.

Harry's Dolci (Fondamenta San Biagio, Giudecca island) An off shoot of Harry's Bar and serving similar fare at lower prices. Moderate.

Locanda Montin (Fondamenta di Borgo, Dorsoduro) An upmarket restaurant with outdoor tables and a lively atmosphere. Expensive.

Gelati Nico (Fondamenta delle Zattere, Dorsoduro) Offers possibly the best *gelati* in Venice and great views of the Canale della Giudecca.

St Mark's Square

St Mark's

Children's Venice

Venice will be a hit with any children old enough to walk its traffic-free streets, providing almost continual diversion. The only problem is to avoid getting lost. A ride on a gondola, *vaporetto* or *traghetto* is guaranteed to amuse; any ice-cream in any Venetian square will provide plenty of live entertainment.

Transport in Venice

Transport within the city is by boat or on foot, both pleasantly effortless compared with other Italian cities.

Waterbuses (*vaporetti*)

The cumbersome passenger-carrying boats which ply the Grand Canal and other main routes. There is a flat fare for tickets which are available from boarding-places, *tabacchini* and other outlets with ACTV signs outside, and the ACTV offices in Piazzale Roma and Ramo dei Fusari, where route maps can also be obtained. Return fares are cheaper than two singles, and you can buy unlimited-travel passes valid for 24 or 72 hours. Normally you should not have to wait more than 10 or 15 minutes for a *vaporetto*.

Useful *vaporetto* routes

Number 1: slow, but good for a thorough exploration of the Grand Canal. Going from Piazzale Roma to Piazza San Marco, it calls at every stop on the canal (45 minutes).

Numbers 3 and 4: summer-only routes connecting the rail station with the Grand Canal and San Marco

Number 12: an hourly service from Fondamente Nuove to the islands of Murano, Burano and Torcello

Number 52: from Murano to Piazzale Roma, then Canale della Giudecca, San Marco, across to the Lido and back

Number 82: from the Tronchetto (one of the main car parks near the rail station) down the Grand Canal to San Marco, in the summer going on to the Lido, then round the Canale della Giudecca and back

Traghetti

Short-distance gondolas for quick hops across the Grand Canal, useful for avoiding long roundabout walks to find bridges. Flat fares are paid to the gondolier on boarding.

Watertaxis

A watertaxi (*taxi acqueo*) is a convenient but fairly expensive way to get somewhere fast. Agree on a fare before starting out.

Gondolas

A gondola-ride is a memorable part of the Venice experience – at a price. Although fares are supposed to be regulated, always make sure that everyone (including the gondolier) is clear about the duration and cost of the ride. You can pay less by sharing the fare among up to six passengers. Prices increase after 8 pm, and accompanying singers or musicians cost extra. You can pick up a gondola at various points along the main canals or around San Marco or the rail station. Avoid riding on the lagoon, which can be choppy.

Daytrips from Venice

Chioggia Chioggia is a pleasant two-hour trip by bus and ferry from the Lido: go to sample the seafood, generally much cheaper and better than in Venice itself.

Palladian villas in the Veneto The Veneto – the region which contains the city of Venice – has the highest concentration of architecture by the great Andrea Palladio. Vicenza is the place most associated with Palladio, but his marriage of classical and Renaissance features can be seen in villas scattered throughout the region. His style was to influence for centuries country houses in England and parts of the United States. His most famous building, La Rotonda, lies little more than a mile from Vicenza, which itself is reachable on frequent trains from Venice.

Verona The fabled city of Romeo and Juliet is also renowned for its huge Roman amphitheatre, today the venue for lavish summer opera productions. Other attractions include the church of San Zeno Maggiore, the most ornate Romanesque church in northern Italy, and the Castelvecchio, a restored 14th-century castle now holding one of the region's finest art galleries.

Venice–Padua along the Brenta canal This route to the old university town of Padua is lined by Palladian villas. One of the most impressive is Villa Pisani, an 18th-century building once owned by Napoleon, with frescos by Tiepolo.

Asolo A medieval walled town north-west of Venice, Asolo owes its elegance to an exiled Venetian princess who established a vibrant court here. Visit the Villa Barbaro, a few kilometres outside town – one of Palladio's most brilliant creations, with frescos by Veronese.

Northern Italy

*N*orthern Italy is studded with prosperous and well-preserved former city-states which can boast a dazzling cultural legacy. Good beaches line both Tyrrhenian and Adriatic coasts, with resorts ranging from popular to sophisticated, as well as a relatively undeveloped shoreline.

Galleria Vittorio Emanuele, Milan

Don't miss

Milan
The fashion hub of Italy and a buzzing commercial and cultural centre.
■ The Duomo, a flamboyantly Gothic confection of marble spires and pinnacles in the heart of the city.
■ A drink in the grandiose Galleria Vittorio Emanuele, a busy arcade of smart cafés and restaurants. The plaque of a beast on the pavement is quite worn by people touching its testicles for luck.
■ The opera at La Scala (December–June).
■ Leonardo's *The Last Supper*, in the church of Santa Maria delle Grazie.
■ (Window-)shopping around Via Monte Napoleone.

Cremona The home of the classical violin. Visit the violin collection at the Palazzo Comunale and the Museo Stradivariano.
Pavia A stroll in the historic centre of this medieval university town; visit the extraordinary Certosa, a profusely decorated Carthusian monastery on the outskirts.
Mantua A medieval town; see the vast Palazzo Ducale, with its frescos

by the native-born Mantegna; more frescos appear in the 16th-century Palazzo del Té.
The Lakes A spectacular contrast to the city-centred culture of northern Italy. Glorified by the Romantics, this mountainous region north of Milan continues to exert its spell. Lake Maggiore has the glorious gardens of Isola Bella. Como was praised by Virgil, Wordsworth and Stendahl, and Garda offers a gamut of water-sports. There are numerous smaller lakes and good hiking terrain round about.

Duomo

Tours of the main sights of the north

Cinque Terre

Route 1

A coastal route along the Italian
Riviera to Lucca (car/rail).

San Remo: promenade along the
seafront. The aristocratic Edwardian
atmosphere is softened by the
profusion of flowers for which the
resort is famous.

Genoa: established as a
Mediterranean power in the 13th
century, Genoa remains Italy's most
important commercial port with a
lively feel and labyrinthine street
markets.

Portofino: at the end of an
enchanting coast road, take a break
in one of Italy's most stylish resorts.

Cinque Terre: five cliff-clinging
villages connected by a dramatic
footpath with wonderful views over
the sea.

Lucca: a Tuscan walled town par
excellence. See the exuberant Pisan-
Romanesque cathedral, stroll in the
elegant gardens of the Palazzo
Pfanner and wander along the
formidable 17th-century ramparts.

Portofino

Route 2
An inland route along the Po Valley following the old Roman Via Aemilia (car / rail).

Ravenna: highlights of the Roman and Byzantine mosaics are the Tomb of Galla Placidia and the San Vitale church.

Duomo, Orvieto

Parma: famous for its ham and parmesan; the Baptistery perfectly sets off the 12th-century Duomo in the heart of the elegant old town.

Modena: visit the Galleria Estense, comprising art treasures salvaged from the city of Ferrara, when the latter was absorbed by the Papal States.

Bologna: an ancient university town and the gastronomic capital of Italy. Piazza Maggiore is one of the great Italian squares.

Ferrara: one of Europe's finest Renaissance towns dominated by the massive, moated Castello Estense: see also the smaller-scale Renaissance *palazzi* scattered about the quiet streets.

Rimini: one of Europe's premier beach resorts, especially popular with the younger clubbing crowds.

Route 3
A circular route through Umbria, the 'green heart of Italy' (car).

Perugia: an imposing medieval city whose winding passageways dive and climb dramatically beneath arches and grey-walled *palazzi*. The Galleria Nazionale in the 400-year-old Palazzo della Pilotta is one of the region's best collections of Renaissance art.

Gubbio: a tiny town of twisting lanes and magnificent views, best appreciated from the perfectly sited Piazza della Signoria.

Assisi: the Basilica di San Francesco houses the frescos damaged in the 1997 earthquake.

Spoleto: an engaging jumble of steps and steep streets, with a 14th-century viaduct offering serene views. Sample the local specialities – truffles and wild mushrooms.

Orvieto: the resplendent facade of the Romanesque-Gothic Duomo dominates the spur of rock on which the town stands.

Orvieto

Southern Italy

Southern Italy is radically different from the north, characterized by a fiercer climate, a harsh landscape and sparse industry. Along the coasts, the beaches are amongst the best in Italy, and quieter, with less of the tourist crush. Culturally, the tone is set by the Baroque in all its manifestations, with a strong infusion of Arab and Norman styles, reflecting the south's distinct history and development.

Fresco from Pompeii

Don't miss

Bay of Naples

Naples
An exuberant city, in its culture and atmosphere, Naples is worth spending time in.

■ The historic centre, around Spaccanapoli. Soak up the street life, shop in the markets and pause in the churches and piazzas.

■ The Archaeological Museum, including frescos from Pompeii and the Farnese Bull sculpture.

■ Capodimonte, a Bourbon royal palace in extensive grounds. The roof terrace has stunning views.

■ The church of Santa Chiara, holding the tombs of Angevin kings; the adjoining cloisters are embellished by majolica tiles depicting rural life painted by the nuns.

■ The Santa Lucia waterfront, a romantic, if expensive, place to eat and be serenaded.

Caserta The Bourbon palace here is a somewhat down-at-heel version of the palace of Versailles, with sweeping staircases, sumptuous royal apartments and acres of parkland

Pompeii and Herculaneum Despite the hordes of fellow tourists, there is real pleasure in wandering around these excavated streets to get an authentic taste of Roman provincial life. Not to be missed.

Paestum One of Europe's greatest classical temple complexes, but relatively unvisited, an hour south of Salerno. Spring is the best time to come, when the site is sprinkled with wild flowers.

Matera A town which mixes Baroque opulence with rugged beauty, perched on the edge of a ravine in Basilicata.

Venosa Remains from diverse eras dot Horace's birthplace in Basilicata.

Positano

including a Roman amphitheatre, a ruined early medieval abbey and a 16th-century cathedral and castle.

The Gargano Sandy beaches are the best reason to come to this promontory in Puglia.

Tours of the main sights of the south

Route 1
Along the scenic Amalfi coast (car).

Salerno: a port chiefly notable for its 11th-century Duomo.

Amalfi: once one of Italy's principal maritime powers, now a chic resort.

Ravello: a hilltop eyrie, whose lush gardens provide exhilarating views over the sea.

Positano: a much-photographed cascade of white-washed houses plunging down a steep hillside to the sea.

Sorrento: draped with semi-tropical vegetation, the clifftop town enjoys glittering views out to the islands in the Bay of Naples.

Capri: take an *aliscafo* (hydrofoil) to this deluxe holiday island, little spoiled by its long popularity. The views from Tiberius's Villa Jovis are worth the half-hour walk from the main town.

Ravello

19

Route 2
From the Adriatic coast into the heart of Puglia (car/rail).

Lecce: a gem of southern Baroque architecture, where the façades of such churches as the Basilica di

Calabria

Bari: capital of the Puglia region and a marvellous place to eat fish. Wander through the maze of streets in the old town, designed deliberately to confuse foreign raiders.
Alberobello: centre of the *trulli* region, it is dotted with these strange dwellings with their conical roofs painted with arcane symbols.
Martina Franca: a Baroque town with a strong Spanish feel – ornate balconies and graceful piazzas.
Taranto: visit the Museo Archeologico, main repository for the wealth of finds from Magna Graecia excavated in the area.
Brindisi: an antique column marks the end-point of the Via Appia. The town is still a thriving commercial port.

Sant'Oronzo and the harmonious Piazza del Duomo show off the pliable local sandstone at its best

Route 3
From one of the major sites of Magna Graecia on the Ionian coast to the tip of the Italian boot (car/rail).
Metaponto: the extensive site of the 8th-century Greek city; see the museum where many of the finds are displayed.
Rossano: see the Codex Purpureus, a beautifully illustrated 6th-century text of the gospels in Greek, and the tiny church of San Marco, one of the loveliest Byzantine relics in southern Italy.
Cosenza: Calabria's most interesting city, with a Swabian castle perched above a compact Old Town. Cosenza is a good base for exploring the Sila, where a national park offers excellent skiing and walking routes.
The Tropea peninsula: an essential swim-stop.
Reggio Calabria: visit the Museo Nazionale della Magna Grecia, holding finds from various sites dotted along the Calabrian coast, most notably the Riace Bronzes two male figures in a near-perfect state of preservation.

Ravello

Sicily

A visit to Sicily is equivalent to a crash-course in Mediterranean culture. Greeks, Carthaginians, Romans, Arabs, Normans and Spaniards have all left their mark in a string of splendid monuments not to mention the dialect, cuisine and culture. Most of the important sights are to be found on the coast, where the heat of summer is moderated by sea breezes. A mountainous island, Sicily's most singular landmark is Mount Etna, Europe's greatest live volcano.

Temple of Castor and Pollux

Don't miss

Palermo
In spite of neglect, Palermo is a compelling place, preserving rich evidence of every phase of its distinguished past.

■ The Palazzo dei Normanni, the royal palace under the Normans, now the seat of the regional government. In particular, see the mosaicked 12th-century Cappella Palatina, an amalgam of Byzantine, Islamic and Norman styles.

■ The Vuccirìa market, just one of several in this city, having more in common with North African souks than anything European. The word 'Vuccirìa' derives from an Arabic word meaning 'hubbub'.

■ Monte Pellegrino. Walk or take a bus to enjoy wonderful views over the sea and the Conca d'Oro (Golden Shell) – the fertile bowl in which the city lies.

■ The Oratorio di Santa Zita. Site of a recreation of the naval Battle of Lepanto, a stucco masterpiece by Giacomo Serpotta.

■ Monreale. Just outside the city, its cathedral is one of the greatest monuments of the cosmopolitan culture which infused Sicily in the 12th century; see also the cloisters, with Moorish-style arches supported on slender columns, each one unique.

Cefalù More lavish mosaics in the Norman cathedral of this fishing town and tourist resort.

Agrigento The greatest collection of ancient Greek temples outside Greece, arrayed along a ridge overlooking the sea.

Taormina This hilltop resort in the shadow of Etna enjoys breathtaking views over the coast, best admired from the inspired site of the Greek and Roman theatre, a venue for concerts and plays in the summer.

Casale An excavated villa near the inland town of Piazza Armerina contains one of the most impressive Roman remains to be found anywhere, a series of astonishingly intact floor-mosaics.

Siracusa Greek monuments mingle with Renaissance and Baroque noble palaces.

Aeolian Islands Take a hydrofoil from Milazzo to this group of volcanic islands scattered off Sicily's northern coast, and swim off lava-black beaches in beautiful unpolluted waters.

Tours of the main sights of Sicily

Palermo

Taormina

Route 1

Around Sicily's far west, taking in two of the island's most important temple sites (car).

Erice

Segesta: an unfinished Doric temple (5th century BC) occupying a majestic inland site close to the remains of a theatre constructed some 200 years later. Superb views.

Capo San Vito: a fine, sandy beach and exhilarating coastal walks.

Erice: ancient Eryx, has an unspoiled medieval air. The views over the city of Trapani and the Egadi islands are outstanding.

Mozia: an ancient Phoenician stronghold on an island where a small museum holds finds including a graceful Greek torso.

Marsala: see the reconstructed Carthaginian warship; sample the dessert wine produced here.

Selinunte: ancient Selinus, a Greek city devastated by Carthage in 409 BC, with scattered remains of temples.

Route 2

Through south-eastern Sicily, famous for its Baroque towns (car).

Pantalica gorge: a dramatic natural phenomenon used as a vast necropolis by Sicily's prehistoric inhabitants. The rock walls are perforated with over 5000 of the rock-cut tombs.

Noto: the most perfect of the towns built in the wake of the 1693 earthquake, its honey-coloured buildings illustrating Baroque at its best.

Modica: another post-earthquake town, built on two levels. The most striking monument is the church of San Giorgio, at the top of a majestic stairway.

Ragusa: a Baroque reconstruction co-exists alongside the old town, spared by the cataclysm. The glorious three-tiered cathedral stands in the lower, medieval town, known as Ragusa Ibla.

Palazzolo Acreide: holds the little-visited remains of the Greek city, Akrai. The city was on an important trade-route and the site today boasts a well-preserved amphitheatre, the ruins of temples and some tombs.

Caltagirone: a town famed for its ceramics. Climb the flight of 142 steps, each decorated with a different tiled pattern. From here you could continue to the Roman villa outside Piazza Armerina (see p21) or take the fast road to Catania or back to Siracusa (see p21).

Sardinia

Sardinia is far from the bustle of mainland Italy in more ways than one. Life is slower, the people are gentler and the cities more manageable. Italians have known about the wonderful waters and clean sands for years, while jetsetters have been enjoying the Costa Smeralda since the 1960s.

Don't miss

Cagliari The Museo Archeologico is an unmissable stop, mainly for the fascinating spindly sculptures which are among the few surviving artefacts of the prehistoric nuraghic culture.

Su Nuraxi The greatest of the nuraghic remains scattered throughout the island. Once a palace, or possibly a citadel, the ruins still wield a strange power, evoking the grandeur of this enigmatic indigenous civilization.

Nora Phoenicians and later Romans settled this city on the sea-shore, now partly submerged.

Alghero A favourite tourist destination, mainly for the graceful Spanish style that characterizes the alleys and buildings in the old town and the good swimming close by.

The Barbagia The mountainous interior is reckoned to hold the real Sardinia, never conquered by foreign powers and displaying the most majestic landscape.

Costa Smeralda You don't need to stay in the deluxe hotels on this brief stretch of coast to appreciate its stunning natural beauty.

Santa Teresa di Gallura at the northern tip of the island facing Corsica. This is a lively resort surrounded by some of Sardinia's finest beaches.

Rocca Ruja beach

Holidays, festivals and events

Siena

January New Year celebrations often feature fireworks. Holidays: 1 January, 6 January (Epiphany).

February Agrigento, Sicily – the Sagra delle Mandorle in Fiore (Almond-Blossom Festival).

March The period before Ash Wednesday is carnival time. Celebrations are held throughout the country, the most famous being Venice's Carnevale. Other highlights are the celebrations at Viareggio (Tuscany), Ivrea (near Turin) and Acireale and Taormina (both in Sicily).

Easter Holy Week is marked everywhere by solemn processions and re-enactments of the Passion. On Easter Sunday, thousands of people attend the Pope's address in St Peter's Square, Rome; Florence stages a grand firework display in Piazza del Duomo. Holidays: Easter Sunday and Monday.

April 25 Saint Mark's Day is commemorated by a gondola race in Venice. Holiday: Liberation Day.

May-June (even-numbered years) Classical plays performed in the Greek theatre in Siracusa.

May 1 Holiday.

May 5 Gubbio, Umbria – Festa dei Ceri: four teams carrying huge candles race through the streets.

May, last Sunday Gubbio – a crossbow tournament in medieval costume between Gubbio and Sansepolcro.

June–July Spoleto's Festa dei Due Mondi (Two Worlds Festival): a range of performing arts.

June–September (odd-numbered years) The Venice Biennale arts festival.

June 24 Costumed processions in Florence, followed by a football match played according to archaic rules.

July–August Umbria Jazz Festival. Taormina – film festival and classical productions in the Greek/Roman theatre. Martina Franca, Puglia – the Festivale della Valle d'Itria with opera, classical and jazz recitals.

July 2 Siena's Piazza del Campo – a ferocious bareback horse race.

July 11 Palermo – rowdy procession for Palermo's patron saint, Santa Rosalia.

August–September Venice – International Film Festival.

August 15 Ferragosto: fireworks and processions all over Italy. Holiday.

August 16 Siena's horse race re-run (see July).

September, first Sunday Venice (Grand Canal) – parade of boats and Historic Regatta of gondolas. Sansepolcro – rematch of Gubbio–Sansepolcro crossbow tournament (see May).

October 3 and 4 Assisi – St Francis's feast days.

November 1 Holiday.

December 8 Holiday.

Mid-December–mid-January La Befana, a crowded fair in Rome's Piazza Navona, has special attractions for children.

December 25 and 26 Holiday.

Venice, Carnevale masks

Bare necessities

Greetings

Hello	**Ciao**
Good morning	**Buongiorno**
Good afternoon / evening	**Buonasera**
How are things?	**Come va?**
How are you?	**Come sta?**
Fine, how are you?	**Bene, e Lei (come sta)?**
Not bad.	**Non c'è male.**
Goodbye (morning)	**Buongiorno**
Goodbye (evening)	**Buonasera**
Goodbye (all day)	**Arrivederci**
Good night	**Buonanotte**
See you later!	**Ci vediamo!**
See you tomorrow!	**A domani!**
Bye	**Ciao**

Other useful words

Excuse me (to attract attention)	**Scusi**
Excuse me (to get by in a crowded place)	**Permesso**
Please	**Per (favore / piacere)**
Thank you (very much)	**Grazie (mille)**
You're welcome.	**Prego.**
Sorry	**Mi (dispiace / scusi)**
It's all right / It doesn't matter.	**Non importa.**
Don't worry.	**Non si preoccupi.**
Yes / No	**Sì / No**

Is / are there . . .?

Is there a lift?	**C'è l'ascensore?**
Are there any toilets?	**Ci sono le toilette?**

ASCENSORE

toilette uomini

Where is / are . . . ?

Where's the station?	**Dov'è la stazione?**
Where are the shoes?	**Dove sono le scarpe?**
It's (on the right / on the left / straight on).	**È (a destra / a sinistra / sempre dritto).**
They're at the end / down there.	**Sono là in fondo.**

Do you have any . . . ?

Do you have any prawns?	**Ha gamberetti?**

How much . . . ?

How much does it cost?	**Quanto costa?**
How much do they cost?	**Quanto costano?**
How much are the (strawberries / tomatoes) a kilo?	**Quanto costano (le fragole / i pomodori) al chilo?**
How much is that (altogether)?	**Quant'è (in tutto)?**

I'd like . . .

I'd like a (shirt / melon).	**Vorrei (una camicia / un melone).**
I'd like (a kilo of apples).	**Mi dà (un chilo di mele).**

Getting things straight

Pardon?	**Come scusi? / Prego?**
Could you say that again?	**Può ripetere?**
More slowly, please.	**Più lentamente, per favore.**
I (don't) understand.	**(Non) capisco.**
Do you understand?	**Capisce?**
How do you spell it?	**Come si scrive?**
Can you write it down, please?	**Può scriverlo, per favore?**
What does it mean?	**Che cosa vuol dire?**
I don't know.	**Non lo so.**

About yourself

My name is . . .	**Mi chiamo . . .**
I'm (Mr / Mrs / Miss) . . .	**Sono (il signor / la signora / la signorina) . . .**
How do you do?	**Piacere.**
I'm from . . .	**Sono di . . .**
I'm Irish.	**Sono irlandese.**
I work in an office.	**Sono impiegato/a.**
I study economics.	**Studio economia.**
I speak a little Italian.	**Parlo un po' d'italiano.**
I'm here on (holiday / business).	**Sono qui (in vacanza / per affari).**
So am I.	**Anch'io.**
I'm staying for a week.	**Mi fermo una settimana.**

About other people

What's your name?	**Come si chiama?**
This is (Mr . . . / my husband / my colleague [male]).	**Questo è (il signor . . . / mio marito / il mio collega).**
This is (Mrs . . . / my wife / my colleague [female]).	**Questa è (la signora . . . / mia moglie / la mia collega).**
May I introduce (Mr / Mrs) . . . ?	**Le presento (il signor / la signora) . . .**
Where are you from?	**Di dov'è?**
Are you English?	**Lei è inglese?**
What do you do for a living?	**Che lavoro fa?**
Do you speak English?	**Parla inglese?**
Are you here on holiday?	**È qui in vacanza?**
How long are you staying for?	**Quanto (tempo) si ferma?**

Money

Before the introduction of the euro in 2002, the currency in Italy was the lira (plural lire).

un euro   due euro   100 euro
(see p30 for numbers)

Changing money

I'd like to change (£100 / $100 / Aus $100).	**Vorrei cambiare cento (sterline / dollari / dollari australiani).**
Here you are.	**Ecco.**
What's the exchange rate, please?	**Quant'è il cambio, per favore?**
What's the commission charge?	**Quant'è la commissione?**

Mi fa vedere il passaporto?	May I see your passport?
La commissione è . . .	The commission charge is . . .

The time

What time is it?	**Che (ora è / ore sono?)**
It's (midday / midnight).	**È (mezzogiorno / mezzanotte).**
It's one o'clock.	**È l'una.**
It's (two / three) o'clock . . .	**Sono le (due / tre) . . .**
It's ten past one.	**È l'una e dieci.**
It's quarter past two.	**Sono le due e un quarto.**
It's half past three.	**Sono le tre e mezza.**
It's quarter to four.	**Sono le quattro meno un quarto.**
It's 20 to six.	**Sono le sei meno venti.**
What time do you (open / close)?	**A che ora (apre / chiude)?**
What time does it (leave / arrive)?	**A che ora (parte / arriva)?**
At two o'clock.	**Alle due.**

Alphabet

In Italian, the letters of the alphabet are pronounced as follows.

A (ah)	**N** (ehnnay)
B (bee)	**O** (o)
C (chee)	**P** (pee)
D (dee)	**Q** (koo)
E (ay)	**R** (ehrray)
F (ehffay)	**S** (ehssay)
G (jee)	**T** (tee)
H (ahkkah)	**U** (oo)
I (ee)	**V** (voo)
J (ee lunga)	**W** (doppia voo)
K (kappa)	**X** (eecs)
L (ehllay)	**Y** (ee greca)
M (ehmmay)	**Z** (dzaytah)

Colours

black	**nero/a**
blue	**blu**
brown	**marrone**
green	**verde**
grey	**grigio/a**
orange	**arancio**
pink	**rosa**
purple	**viola**
red	**rosso/a**
white	**bianco/a**
yellow	**giallo/a**

light / dark **chiaro / scuro**

Numbers

0	**zero**	26	**ventisei**
1	**uno**	27	**ventisette**
2	**due**	28	**ventotto**
3	**tre**	29	**ventinove**
4	**quattro**	30	**trenta**
5	**cinque**	40	**quaranta**
6	**sei**	50	**cinquanta**
7	**sette**	60	**sessanta**
8	**otto**	70	**settanta**
9	**nove**	80	**ottanta**
10	**dieci**	90	**novanta**
11	**undici**	100	**cento**
12	**dodici**	101	**centouno**
13	**tredici**	110	**centodieci**
14	**quattordici**	200	**duecento**
15	**quindici**	1000	**mille**
16	**sedici**	1102	**millecentodue**
17	**diciassette**	2000	**duemila**
18	**diciotto**	2102	**duemilacento due**
19	**diciannove**		
20	**venti**	3000	**tremila**
21	**ventuno**	10.000	**diecimila**
22	**ventidue**	15.000	**quindicimila**
23	**ventitré**	100.000	**centomila**
24	**ventiquattro**	1.000.000	**un milione**
25	**venticinque**		

Ordinal numbers

1st	**primo/a**	7th	**settimo/a**
2nd	**secondo/a**	8th	**ottavo/a**
3rd	**terzo/a**	9th	**nono/a**
4th	**quarto/a**	10th	**decimo/a**
5th	**quinto/a**	11th	**undicesimo/a**
6th	**sesto/a**	12th	**dodicesimo/a**

Countries and nationalities

Australia	**Australia: australiano/a**
Austria	**Austria: austriaco/a**
Belgium	**Belgio: belga**
Canada	**Canada: canadese**
China	**Cina: cinese**
Denmark	**Danimarca: danese**
England	**Inghilterra: inglese**
Finland	**Finlandia: finlandese**
France	**Francia: francese**
Germany	**Germania: tedesco / a**
Great Britain	**Gran Bretagna: britannico/a**
Greece	**Grecia: greco/a**
India	**India: indiano/a**
Ireland	**Irlanda: irlandese**
Italy	**Italia: italiano/a**
Japan	**Giappone: giapponese**
Luxemburg	**Lussemburgo: lussemburghese**
Netherlands/Holland	**Olanda: olandese**
New Zealand	**Nuova Zelanda: neozelandese**
Northern Ireland	**l'Irlanda del Nord: irlandese**
Norway	**Norvegia: norvegese**
Portugal	**Portogallo: portoghese**
Russia	**Russia: russo/a**
Scotland	**Scozia: scozzese**
South Africa	**Sudafrica: sudafricano/a**
Spain	**Spagna: spagnolo/a**
Sweden	**Svizzera: svizzero/a**
Switzerland	**Svezia: svedese**
United States/ America	**gli Stati Uniti: americano/a**
Wales	**Galles: gallese**

Days

Monday	**lunedì**	Saturday	**sabato**
Tuesday	**martedì**	Sunday	**domenica**
Wednesday	**mercoledì**	yesterday	**Ieri**
Thursday	**giovedì**	today	**oggi**
Friday	**venerdì**	tomorrow	**domani**

Months

January	**gennaio**	July	**luglio**
February	**febbraio**	August	**agosto**
March	**marzo**	September	**settembre**
April	**aprile**	October	**ottobre**
May	**maggio**	November	**novembre**
June	**giugno**	December	**dicembre**

Language works

Greetings

1 Small talk in the hotel
- Lei è inglese?
- □ Sì, sono di Durham e lei di dov'è?
- Io sono di Verona. Mi chiamo Bruni. Piacere.
- □ Piacere – Walker.
- Quanto si ferma qui a Bellagio?
- □ Una settimana.
- Anch'io.

Signor Bruni asks you whether you are Scottish: true/false

2 More talk
- Buongiorno, come va?
- □ Buongiorno, bene grazie, e lei?
- Bene, bene . . . Signor Bruni, che lavoro fa?
- □ Sono impiegato.
- Ahh, sì.
- □ E lei, che lavoro fa?
- Studio economia e italiano.

What does Signor Bruni do for a living?

Money

3 Changing money
- Buongiorno, vorrei cambiare cento sterline.
- □ Mi fa vedere il passaporto?
- Ecco. . . . Quant'è il cambio per favore?
- □ Una sterlina 2550 lire.

What's the exchange rate?

Try it out

Crossword

Across

3 Goodbye
6 A greeting to use when you're introduced to an Italian
7 Hello (on the phone)
8 Thank you

Down

1 To get someone's attention
2 You're in Italy, not on business but on . . .
4 An informal greeting
5 You're welcome!

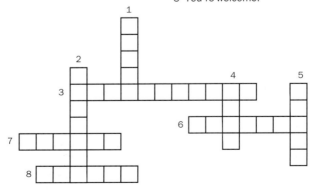

Questions & answers

Match the questions and the answers.

1 Dov'è la stazione?
   a Bene, grazie, e lei?
2 Quando è aperta la banca?
   b Sono di Venezia.
3 Di dov'è lei?
   c È sempre dritto.
4 Come sta?
   d Sette mila lire.
5 Quanto costa?
   e Alle due e mezza.

As if you were there

1 Introduce yourself.
2 Introduce Mr Smith to Mrs Rossi.
3 Ask Mrs Rossi how to spell Rossi.
4 Ask Mrs Rossi to repeat what she said.
5 Ask Mrs Rossi whether she speaks any English.
6 Say goodbye formally (it's 5 pm).

Sound Check

a, **i**, and **u** are very straight forward.

a   like 'a' in 'park'
    casa   casa

i   like 'ee' in 'sheep'
    vino   veeno

u   like 'oo' in 'tool'
    uva   oova

e and **o** are are slightly more complicated, as they can have two different pronunciations.

e   open sound, like 'e' in 'pen' or 'è' in French word 'première'
    terra   tèrra
    closed sound, like 'a' in 'base' or 'é' in French word 'café'
    pera   péra

o   open sound, like 'o' in 'hot'
    pollo   pollo
    closed sound, like 'oa' in 'load'
    noce   noache

It is difficult to give a general rule on pronunciation for these letters, so it is a good idea to learn it for each new word as you go along.

Getting around

Airports

All the airports have regular bus connections to the centre, except for Rome Fiumicino (Leonardo da Vinci airport) which is connected by train. Taxi rates can be fairly steep.

Driving

Hiring a car is relatively expensive: arrange a fly-drive deal before leaving or check out smaller rental operators where you're staying – prices are generally cheaper. Scooter hire is also a possibility for short distances.

Note that driving in Italy can be a stressful, as well as expensive, experience, with congestion and lack of parking a problem. Petty car-crime is also common.

Road types

A or E roads *Autostrade* (motorways) for which you pay (take a ticket on joining the motorway, pay on exit). Speed limit: 80mph, 70mph for cars with engines of less than 1100cc and 60mph for campers.

S or SS roads *Superstrade* or *Strade Statali* (main trunk roads) – one or two lanes. Speed limit: 70mph on dual carriageways, 55mph on all other roads.
Urban roads Speed limit: 30mph.
Documentation All car documentation should be carried at all times, including your driving licence. A green card is generally advisable.
Petrol Prices are higher than in most other European countries
Super – four-star
(Benzina)Senza-Piombo / Senza-PB – unleaded
Gasolio – diesel
Petrol stations open 7 am–12.30 pm and 3.30–7.30 pm, except Sunday (mornings only). On motorways they are open 24 hours. Most towns have automatic pumps which accept L10.000 and L50.000 notes at all hours.
Breakdowns The Automobile Club d'Italia (ACI) operates an emergency breakdown service, though charges are high for non-members or those whose motoring clubs at home do not have a reciprocal agreement.

| Voli Nazionali Domestic Flights | Autonoleggi Rent a car |
| Partenze Internazionali International Departures | Stazione FS Railway Station |

 I'd like to hire a car.
Vorrei noleggiare una macchina.

divieto di sosta

Trains

Italian rail is a reliable, convenient and cheap way to cover long distances. Reservation is recommended.

Train types
Pendolino Fastest and most expensive trains; must be reserved in advance, supplement also payable.
Intercity Fast trains linking major cities; seat-reservation necessary; supplement payable before boarding.
Interregionale, Espresso and Diretto The most common trains, currently referred to by all three names; do not stop at local stations.
Regionale and Locale Local trains, covering shorter distances and stopping at every station.

Tickets
Tickets can be purchased at the station or at some travel agents, and must be punched at special machines on or near the platforms shortly before boarding. Return tickets are valid for up to three days (the return ticket price is the same as two singles).

Some trains don't run all the time: check the timetable for restrictions, marked *stagionale* or *periodico*.

Where do I need to get off?
Dove devo scendere?

Discounts and passes
■ Toddlers under 4 travel for free.
■ Children under 12 pay 50% of the full fare.
Further discounts may be available. Ask for details of:
■ *Carta Verde* (under-26)
■ *Carta Famiglia* (family of up to 4)
■ *Carta d'Argento* (over-60)
■ Passes for specified periods of time/distance

Coaches

Travel by coach (*pullman*) tends to be pricier than train-travel, though schedules are generally more reliable. Major towns have a central *autostazione* (bus station). In smaller towns, you may have to purchase tickets at a bar near the coach-stop. Sometimes you can buy tickets on board.

When does the bus to Venice leave?
A che ora parte l'autobus per Venezia?

Other options

Taxis

Useful for crossing the city quickly, but they can be expensive, especially for journeys to or from airports. Choose only official taxis (those with 'Taxi' on the roof) and fix a price beforehand if travelling any distance. Supplements are added for luggage, being called by telephone, out-of-town rides and rides on Sundays / public holidays / at night.

Cycling

This is a common form of transport in the north of Italy. As a rule, avoid much-travelled roads, and make sure you can be seen.

Ferries and hydrofoils

The ferry (*traghetto*) and hydrofoil (*aliscafo*) and other craft are an integral part of the Italian transport system, essential for reaching the many outlying islands.

Getting to Sicily

Ferry to Palermo from Naples or Sardinia, or to Messina from Villa San Giovanni, north of Reggio Calabria. Trains are transported on the Messina ferry and continue their journey in Sicily. Other ferries from here take cars and foot-passengers.

Routes to the islands

If you are travelling to Capri, Ischia or the Aeolian Islands, you can choose between a ferry or the much faster hydrofoil. The hydrofoil costs around twice as much as the ferry. There are departures from Naples or Sorrento for Capri or Ischia, and from Naples, Palermo or Messina for the Aeolians. Ferries for the Aeolians leave from Milazzo, a 40-minute bus-ride from Messina.

Other routes

Genoa, Livorno, Civitavecchia (near Rome), Naples and Palermo have services to Sardinia. Both ferries and hydrofoils link the smaller islands around Sicily's coast, leaving from Palermo, Agrigento and Trapani.

City Transport

Buses, trams and funiculars

City buses and trams are cheap and frequent, though they can also be unbearably crowded, and in summer you may prefer to walk. There is also an efficient night service in most towns, with hourly departures. Funiculars are a useful way of getting up or down quickly in places like Naples or Orvieto.

Tickets (*biglietti*) must be purchased before boarding and immediately validated inside the bus (*autobus*), tram or funicular. Usually, the same ticket can be used on the bus, tram, funicular and underground and is valid for 60 or 75 minutes after being stamped (but check locally). They are obtainable from *tabacchini* and some news-vendors and bars, as well as from kiosks at bus stations. You can buy blocks of tickets, or, in some places, one-day passes.

Metropolitana

Rome, Naples and Milan all have useful (if limited) underground railway systems. Milan has three lines meeting at the Stazione Centrale, while Rome has just two lines – again converging on the main rail station, Termini – and Naples only one. Services stop at around 11 pm. Note that Naples also has a useful private railway line linking Herculaneum, Pompeii and Sorrento.

Excuse me, which way is the tourist office?

Scusi, dov'è l'ufficio del turismo?

Phrasemaker

Asking the way

Excuse me	**Scusi**
Which way is the (station / tourist office)?	**Dov'è (la stazione / l'ufficio del turismo)?**
Is it far?	**È lontano?**
Is there a (bank / car-park) near here?	**C'è (una banca / un parcheggio) qui vicino?**
Are there any (toilets / shops) near here?	**Ci sono (toilette / negozi) qui vicino?**
Is this the right way to the (town centre / airport)?	**Questa è la strada per (il centro / l'aeroporto)?**
Dunque . . . / Allora . . .	Well . . . / Right . . .
È là.	There it is / It's over there.
A (destra / sinistra)	On the (right / left)
Giri a (destra / sinistra).	Turn (right / left).
Vada sempre dritto.	Carry straight on.
Poi attraversi (il ponte / la strada).	Then cross the (bridge / road).
La (prima / seconda) a destra	(First / second) on the right
Dopo il semaforo	After the traffic lights
Fino all'incrocio	As far as the crossroads
A 100 metri	100 metres away
In fondo alla strada	At the end of the street
(Dietro l' / All') angolo	(Round / On) the corner
È abbastanza (vicino / lontano)	It's quite (near / far away)
Di fronte (al museo / alla chiesa)	Opposite the (museum / church)
Dietro la banca	Behind the bank

Places in a town

beach	**la spiaggia**	port	**il porto**
bridge	**il ponte**	railway	**la stazione**
bus station	**la stazione degli autobus**	station	**ferroviaria**
		shops	**i negozi**
bus stop	**la fermata dell'autobus**	square	**la piazza**
		stadium	**lo stadio**
castle	**il castello**	statue	**la statua**
cathedral	**la cattedrale**	street	**la via**
chemist's	**la farmacia**	swimming pool	**la piscina**
church	**la chiesa**	toilets	**le toilette**
hospital	**l'ospedale (m.)**	town walls	**le mura**
market	**il mercato**	water bus stop	**l'imbarcadero**
museum	**il museo**	underground	**la stazione**
palace	**il palazzo**	station	**della**
park	**il parco**		**metropolitana**
police station	**la questura**		

Pedestrian signs

Hiring a car or bike

I'd like to hire a (car / bike).	**Vorrei noleggiare una (macchina / bicicletta).**
a (small / medium / big) car	**una macchina (piccola / media / grande)**
for (three days / a week)	**per (tre giorni / una settimana)**
How much is it per (day / week)?	**Quanto costa (al giorno / alla settimana)?**
Is insurance included?	**È inclusa l'assicurazione?**

Per quanto tempo?	For how long?
Mi fa vedere (la patente / il passaporto), per favore?	Can I see your (driving licence / passport), please?
La cauzione è di . . . lire.	The deposit is . . . lira.
	(more on cars on p34)

Buying petrol

30 litres of . . .	**Trenta litri di . . .**
4-star / unleaded / diesel	**Super / benzina senza piombo / gasolio**
Fill it up, please.	**Il pieno, per favore.**
Can you check the (tyres / water / oil)?	**Mi controlla (le gomme / l'acqua / l'olio)?**

Road signs

Centro	City centre	**Senso unico**	One-way
Parcheggio (gratuito / a pagamento)	(Free / paying) parking	**Nord**	North
		Sud	South
		Autostrada	Motorway
Giorni feriali	Weekdays	**Divieto di sosta**	No parking
Giorni festivi	Sundays and holidays	**Rallentare**	Reduce speed
		Lavori in corso	Road works
Accostare a destra	Keep right	**Divieto di sorpasso**	No overtaking
Precedenza	Priority		
Vicolo cieco	Dead end		
Deviazione	Diversion		

Roadside information

Is this the road to . . .?	**Questa è la strada per . . .?**
How far is it to . . .?	**Quanto è distante . . .?**
Where is . . .?	**Per . . .?**

Using the underground

A single, please	**Un biglietto, per favore**
A book of tickets	**Un blocchetto di biglietti**
Which line goes to . . .?	**Che linea per . . .?**
Does this train go to . . .?	**Questo treno va a . . .?**

Prenda (la linea / il numero) . . .	Take (line / number) . . .
Deve (cambiare / scendere) alla prossima.	You need to (change / get off) at the next stop.

Getting information on trains and buses

Are there (buses / trains) to . . .?	**Ci sono (autobus / treni) per . . .?**
What time does the bus (leave / arrive)?	**A che ora (parte / arriva) l'autobus?**
What time does the next one leave?	**A che ora parte il prossimo?**
From which platform?	**Da che binario?**
Is it direct?	**È diretto?**
What time is the connection?	**A che ora è la coincidenza?**
Have you got a timetable?	**Ha un orario?**
Does this bus go to . . . ?	**Questo autobus va a . . . ?**
Where do I need to get off?	**Dove devo scendere?**

C'è (un treno / una corriera) ogni ora.	There's a (train / coach) every hour.
Fra/Tra (un quarto d'ora / mezz'ora)	In (a quarter of an hour / half an hour)
Deve (cambiare / scendere) fra due fermate.	You have to (change / get off) in two stops.
Le faccio vedere.	I'll show you.

Buying a ticket

Where is the ticket office, please?	**Dov'è la biglietteria, per favore?**
A (single / return) to . . .	**Un biglietto (solo andata / andata e ritorno) per . . .**
For two adults and one child	**Per due adulti e un bambino**
1st / 2nd class	**Prima / seconda classe**
I'd like to reserve a (seat / couchette).	**Vorrei prenotare (un posto / una cuccetta).**

Fumatori o non-fumatori?	Smoking or non-smoking?
. . . lire di supplemento intercity	an intercity supplement of . . . lira

Transport

bicycle	**la bicicletta**		train	**il treno**
boat	**il battello**		tram	**il tram**
bus	**l'autobus**		underground	**la metro-politana**
car	**la macchina**			
coach	**la corriera / il pullman**		waterbus	**il vaporetto**
ferry	**il traghetto**			
flight	**il volo**			
hydrofoil	**l'aliscafo**			
motorbike	**la moto**			
plane	**l'aereo**			
scooter	**la vespa**			
taxi	**il taxi**			

Signs

Arrivi	Arrivals	**Ufficio oggetti smarriti**	Lost property
Partenze	Departures		
Convalidare il biglietto	Validate your ticket	**Servizio taxi**	Taxi service
		Acqua potabile	Drinking water
Binario	Platform	**Accettazione**	Check-in
Vietato attraversare i binari	Do not cross the tracks	**Controllo di sicurezza**	Security check
Vietato sporgersi dal finestrino	Do not lean out of the window	**Controllo passaporti**	Passport control
Vietato fumare	No smoking	**Dogana**	Customs
Deposito bagagli	Left-luggage office	**Uscita**	Gate
		Cambio	Exchange

Train travel

compartment	**lo scompartimento**
restaurant car	**la vettura ristorante**
sleeping car	**il vagone letto**
suitcase	**la valigia**
taxi rank	**il posteggio di taxi**
timetable	**l'orario**
trolley (deposit / collect) luggage	**il carrello (depositare / ritirare) i bagagli**
reserve a couchette	**prenotare una cuccetta**

Taking a taxi

Is there a taxi rank near here?	**C'è un posteggio di taxi qui vicino?**
To the airport, please.	**L'aeroporto, per favore.**
To this address, please.	**Questo indirizzo, per favore.**
Is it far?	**È lontano?**
How long will it take?	**Quanto tempo ci vuole?**
How much will it be?	**Quanto costa?**
Keep the change.	**Tenga il resto.**
This is for you.	**Questo è per lei.**
Could I have a receipt, please?	**Mi dà la ricevuta, per favore?**
Va bene	Fine

Language works

Asking the way

1 You want to go to the station
- **Scusi, dov'è la stazione?**
- □ **Allora, vada sempre dritto, dopo il semaforo la seconda a destra.**
- **È lontano?**
- □ **No, a 100 metri.**

The station is straight on, then on the left after the traffic lights: true/false

Hiring a car or bike

2 You'll be asked to leave a deposit
- **Buongiorno, vorrei noleggiare una macchina media, una Panda. Quanto costa al giorno?**
- □ **. . . 90.000 al giorno. Per quanto tempo?**
- **Per una settimana. È inclusa l'assicurazione?**
- □ **Sì. C'è una cauzione di 350.000 lire.**

The car costs 90.000 lira a day: true/false

Getting information on trains and buses

3 Checking with the driver
- **Questo autobus va a Venezia?**
- □ **Sì.**
- **Dove devo scendere?**
- □ **Deve scendere fra due fermate.**

You need to get off at the next stop: true/false

Taking a taxi

4 You're going to the airport
- **L'aeroporto, per favore. Quanto costa?**
- □ **45.000.**
- **Quanto tempo ci vuole?**
- □ **Venti minuti.**

  . . .
- □ **45.000.**
- **Ecco – e questo è per lei. Mi dà la ricevuta, per favore?**

To get to the airport takes:
5 minutes / 10 minutes / 20 minutes

Try it out

Crossword

Across

2 A che ora è la _____?
3 Ecco il passaporto e la _____.
5 Quanto costa un _____?
6 Dopo il _____ a destra.
9 C'è una _____ qui vicino?
10 È inclusa l' _____.

Down

1 Da che _____ parte?
4 Quanto _____ ci vuole?
7 Dov'è la _____ dell'autobus?
8 Andata o andata e _____?

As if you were there

- **Prego?**
- □ (Ask for two return tickets to Venice.)
- **42.800 e 5000 lire di supplemento intercity.**
- □ (Ask what time the train leaves.)
- **Alle 10.08.**
- □ (Ask whether it is a direct train.)
- **No, deve cambiare a Padova.**
- □ (Ask what time the connection is.)
- **Dunque, il treno arriva a Padova alle 12.30 e la coincidenza è alle 13.05.**
- □ (Thank him.)

Sound Check

c is pronounced in two ways, depending on the letter which follows it

c + e or **i**	like 'ch' in 'church'
cena	chena
cinque	cheenkwe

c + anything else	like 'c' in 'cool'
camera	kamera
costano	kostano
bicchiere	beekyere
che	ke

Practise on these words:
carne, centro, chi, città, nocciola, riscaldamento

Somewhere to stay

At a glance

■ Book beforehand in major resorts and in summer.
■ Contact your local Italian tourist board for a list of hotels, apartments, *agriturismo* facilities and campsites.
■ If you do not have a reservation, ask for advice at a local tourist office. They can also arrange accommodation for you, usually without charge.

Types of accommodation

Italy has a good range of accommodation. Most of the coastal resorts offer either hotel, camping, self-catering or private rooms; tourist offices can provide a comprehensive list of local lodgings with prices and facilities, and can phone for you to check availability and sometimes make reservations.

❗ Do you have a double room for two nights?
🗣 Ha una camera doppia per due notti?

Catering for children

All types of accommodation cater for children of all ages, and will install an extra bed in your room for an extra 30-40% of the price of the room.

Hotels

Hotel accommodation is categorized by stars – from one (cheapest) to five (most expensive). Three or more stars will generally include a telephone and television and en suite facilities.

In high season, many hotels insist on visitors paying for half- or full-board. Avoid rates which include breakfast, if you can: you'll find it cheaper and better in local bars.

❗ How much is it per night?
🗣 Quanto costa per una notte?

Self-catering and *agriturismo*

Self-catering can be a much cheaper and more satisfying alternative to hotel accommodation. Villas and apartments are best booked through an agency before leaving. In the countryside, the *agriturismo* scheme offers self-catering cottage or farmhouse holidays. The tourist office can supply you with a list of apartments in towns or *agriturismo* facilities.

> ❗ What time is breakfast?
> **A che ora è la prima colazione?**

Youth hostels, *rifugi* and campsites

Northern Italy has a good distribution of youth hostels, but they are sparse south of Rome. Hostels are usually located outside the city centres, a bus ride away. In most cases you must hold a current IYHF card (sometimes obtainable from the hostel) or take out temporary membership; in some private hostels this is not necessary.

Hikers will appreciate the mountain huts (*rifugi*) strung along walking routes, often in highly scenic locations. Ask at the tourist office about availability and terms, or contact the Club Alpino Italiano at Via Fonseca Pimentel 7, Milan 20127, (02) 2614 1378.

Camping is a popular option, especially on the coasts. Sites can become extremely crowded in summer. Some have huts or small bungalows for rent, and most have bars, restaurants and shops; pools and discotheques are often found in the bigger ones. The local tourist office will have a list of sites in the vicinity. It is best to phone ahead in high season.

Note that many campsites close between September and Easter and that camping outside official sites is illegal.

> ❗ I'd like the bill, please.
> **Vorrei il conto, per favore.**

Phrasemaker
Finding a place

Is there a (hotel / campsite / youth hostel) near here?	**C'è un (albergo / campeggio / ostello) qui vicino?**
Do you have a (single / double) room?	**Ha una camera (singola / doppia)?**
For four people – two adults and two children	**Per quattro persone – due adulti e due bambini**
For two nights	**Per due notti**
How much is it per night?	**Quanto costa per una notte?**
May I see the room?	**Posso vedere la camera?**
Are there any reductions for children?	**Ci sono riduzioni per bambini?**
Do you have anything cheaper?	**Ha qualcosa di meno caro?**
Fine, I'll take it.	**Va bene, la prendo.**
I'll think about it.	**Ci penso.**

Per quante notti?	How many nights?
Per quante persone?	How many people?
Mi dispiace, è tutto occupato.	Sorry, we're full.
I bambini pagano metà.	Children pay half price.

Places to stay

B&B/pension	**la pensione**
hotel	**l' albergo**
motel	**il motel**
youth hostel	**l'ostello**
campsite	**il campeggio**
holiday village	**il villaggio turistico**
(apartments / rooms) with communal kitchen and bathroom	**affittasi (appartamenti / stanze) con cucina e servizi in comune**
self-catering (apartments / villas) to let	**affittasi (appartamenti /villette)**

Specifications

With a (bathroom / shower)	**Con (bagno / doccia)**
With (a double bed / twin beds / a child's bed)	**Con (letto matrimoniale / due letti / un lettino)**
Is breakfast included?	**La prima colazione è inclusa?**

La prima colazione è (inclusa / esclusa).	Breakfast is (included / not included).
La tassa di soggiorno si paga a parte.	The visitor's tax is extra.

Checking in

I have a reservation . . .	**Ho prenotato . . .**
My name's . . .	**Mi chiamo . . .**
Where can I park?	**Dove posso parcheggiare?**

Che nome, per favore?	What name, please?
Mi dà il passaporto, per favore?	Can I have your passport, please?
Può compilare la scheda, per cortesia?	Can you fill in the form, please?
Camera numero . . .	Room number . . .
Il parcheggio è dietro a sinistra.	The car park is at the back on the left.
Che numero di targa ha?	What's your car registration?

Services

What time is (breakfast / dinner)?	**A che ora è la (prima colazione / cena)?**
Is there (a lift / air conditioning)?	**C'è l'(ascensore / aria condizionata)?**
Do you have an (adapter / iron)?	**Ha un (riduttore / ferro da stiro)?**
Where is the (restaurant / bar)?	**Dov'è il (ristorante / bar)?**
How do I get an outside number?	**Come faccio per telefonare fuori?**

Dalle sette e mezza alle dieci e mezza	From 7.30 to 10.30
È al (primo / secondo / terzo) piano.	It's on the (first / second / third) floor.
Faccia lo zero.	Dial zero.

Facilities

air conditioning	**l'aria condizionata**	lift	**l'ascensore**
balcony	**il balcone**	minibar	**il minibar**
bar	**il bar**	phone	**il telefono**
bathroom	**il bagno**	restaurant	**il ristorante**
breakfast	**la prima colazione**	room service	**il servizio in camera**
car park	**il parcheggio**	safe	**la cassaforte**
double room	**una camera matrimoniale**	safe deposit box	**la cassetta di sicurezza**
family room	**con tre/quattro letti**	sauna	**la sauna**
fitness centre	**il centro di fitness**	shower	**la doccia**
games room	**la sala giochi**	single room	**la camera singola**
garden	**il giardino**	swimming pool	**la piscina**
heating	**il riscaldamento**	tennis court	**il campo da tennis**
laundry service	**il servizio lavanderia**	terrace	**la terrazza**
		trouser press	**lo stiracalzoni**
		view of the sea	**la vista sul mare**

Problems

The (telephone / shower) isn't working.	**(Il telefono / La doccia) non funziona.**
There is a problem with . . .	**Ho un problema con . . .**
How do you work the heating?	**Come funziona il riscaldamento?**
There's no (hot water / soap).	**Manca (l'acqua calda / il sapone).**
There are also no (towels / pillows / blankets).	**Mancano anche (gli asciugamani / i cuscini / le coperte).**

Mando qualcuno.	I'll send somebody.
Basta (tirare / spingere / girare)	All you have to do is (pull / push / turn it)
verso (l'alto / il basso)	(upwards / downwards)

In your room

adapter	**il riduttore**	light	**la luce**
air conditioning	**l'aria condizionata**	lock	**la serratura**
		luggage	**i bagagli**
blankets	**le coperte**	phone	**il telefono**
blind	**la persiana**	pillow	**il cuscino**
bulb	**la lampadina**	pillow cases	**le federe**
cold water	**l'acqua fredda**	plug (sink)	**il tappo**
curtain	**la tenda**	radio	**la radio**
door	**la porta**	sheets	**le lenzuola**
hair-dryer	**l'asciugacapelli**	tap	**il rubinetto**
handle	**la maniglia**	television	**il televisore**
heating	**il riscaldamento**	toilet paper	**la carta igienica**
hot water	**l'acqua calda**	towel	**l'asciugamano**
key	**la chiave**	wash basin	**il lavandino**
lamp	**la lampada**	window	**la finestra**

Asking for help

Could I have an alarm call at . . . ?	**Vorrei la sveglia per . . .**
Do you have a plan of the town?	**Ha una pianta della città?**
Is there a (safe / safe deposit box)?	**C'è una (cassaforte / cassetta di sicurezza)?**
Could you recommend a good restaurant?	**Mi può consigliare un buon ristorante?**
Can you order me a taxi?	**Mi può chiamare un taxi?**

Other words to recognize

mezza pensione	half board
pensione completa	full board
la scheda di registrazione	registration form
(bassa / media / alta) stagione	(low / middle / high) season
all'ombra	in the shade
al sole	in the sun

Checking out

I'd like to pay the bill, please.	**Vorrei il conto, per favore.**
Can I pay by (traveller's cheques / credit card / cash)?	**Posso pagare (con traveller's cheque / con la carta di credito / in contanti)?**
I think there's a mistake.	**C'è un errore, credo.**

Qual è il numero della stanza / camera?	What is your room number?
Come vuole pagare?	How would you like to pay?
Può firmare qui, per favore?	Can you sign here, please?
Vediamo . . . Sì, ha ragione.	Let's see . . . Yes, you're right.
Mi scusi.	I'm sorry.

Campsites

Have you got space for a (car / caravan / tent)?	**Ha posto per una (macchina / roulotte / tenda)?**
How much does it cost per (person / day)?	**Quanto si paga (per persona / al giorno)?**
Is there (a laundry / supermarket)?	**C'è (una lavanderia / un supermercato)?**
Where are the (showers / dustbins / toilets)?	**Dove sono (le docce/i cassonetti per la spazzatura/le toilette)?**

Abbiamo una piazzola per tre notti.	We have a pitch free for 3 nights.

Self-catering

I've rented a villa.	**Ho preso in affitto una villetta.**
How does (the heating / water) work?	**Come funziona (il riscaldamento / l'acqua)?**

Language works

Finding a place

1 At the youth hostel
- **Buonasera, ha una camera singola?**
- □ **Mi dispiace, è tutto occupato.**

There's no room available: true/false

2 Looking for a single room
- **Buongiorno, ha una camera singola?**
- □ **Per quante notti?**
- **Per due notti.**
- □ **. . . Sì, ma senza doccia.**
- **Quanto costa?**
- □ **105.500 per notte, la colazione si paga a parte 6000 lire.**
- **Ha qualcosa di meno caro?**
- □ **No, mi dispiace.**
- **Posso vedere la camera?**
- □ **Prego.**

The room available has no shower: true/false
The price of the room including breakfast is 105.500/111.500/115.500

3 Looking for a double room
- **Buonasera, ha una camera doppia?**
- □ **Vediamo, sì, una doppia a due letti.**
- **Quanto viene?**
- □ **123.000.**
- **La prima colazione è inclusa?**
- □ **La colazione si paga a parte 4500 lire per persona.**

The cost of the room including breakfast is . . .

Problems

4 You can't get the shower to work
- **Scusi, come funziona la doccia?**
- □ **Basta tirare e girare verso l'alto.**
- **. . . Non funziona.**
- □ **Mando qualcuno.**
- **Grazie, e mancano anche gli asciugamani.**
- □ **Ecco gli asciugamani.**

To make the shower work, you have to press and turn the control downwards: true/false

Somebody will bring you the towels: true/false

Checking out

5 Spotting a mistake in the bill
- **Vorrei il conto, per favore.**
- □ **Qual è il numero della stanza?**
- **72. Posso pagare con la carta di credito?**
- □ **Certo. Può firmare qui, per favore?**
- **. . . C'è un errore, credo. I bambini pagano metà.**
- □ **Vediamo . . . sì, ha ragione. Mi scusi.**
- **Va bene . . . Vorrei la sveglia per le 6 domani mattina e mi può chiamare un taxi per le 7, per favore?**

What's wrong with the bill?

Try it out

Unscrambling words

Can you find the right word?
1 Scusi, c'è la SASACORTEF nell'albergo?
2 Scusi, manca la TARAC CIANIEGI nella stanza 31.

3 Scusi, come funziona il
  VITEROSELE?
4 Scusi, ho un problema con la
  SARRUTERA.
5 Scusi, mancano gli
  NIMAGASCIUA, nella stanza 32.

Making requests

Complete the sentences using
the prompts.

Example: caravan space
  Ha _____?
  Ha posto per una roulotte?

1 double bed + shower
2 room
3 reductions for children
4 park the car
5 a good restaurant
6 breakfast
7 telephone
8 credit card

1 Ha _____
2 Posso _____?
3 Ci sono _____?
4 Dove _____?
5 Mi _____?
6 A _____?
7 Come _____?
8 Posso _____?

Questions & answers

Match each question with the
correct answer.
1 Ha una camera singola?
  a Due adulti e due bambini.
2 Ha qualcosa di meno caro?
  b No, è esclusa.
3 Che nome per favore?
  c Mi dispiace, è tutto occupato.
4 Quanto costa per notte?
  d Smith.
5 Per quante persone?
  e No, mi dispiace.
6 La prima colazione è inclusa?
  f 74.500.

Sound Check

When **s** comes before **ce**
or **ci**, the pronunciation changes.

s + ce or **ci**   like 'sh' in 'ship'
  ascensore   ashensore
  sciroppo   sheeroppo

Practise on these words:
**asciugamano, lasciare, scelta,
scendere, strisce, uscire**

Buying things

Shops

Shops are generally open Monday–
Saturday 9 am–1 pm and 4–7.30 pm,
though some close on Monday
mornings. Larger shops will accept
credit cards.

    Towns have at least one chemist
open late-night: consult the local
paper or tourist office for details.

Best-value goods

Shoes Especially in Milan and
Florence: highest quality leather
goods in the best designs.
Clothes Italian fashion is world-
famous, and there are plenty of big-
name outlets in every major city.
Naples is also good for cut-price
garments on sale in back streets and
from market stalls.
Ceramics Throughout Italy,
especially Southern Italy and Sicily;
in the north, Emilia-Romagna and
Umbria.
Wine Good value everywhere. The
best selection is at the local *enoteca*
(wine shop), where you can normally
sample before buying.
Olive oil Puglia is one of Europe's
biggest producers.
Woven rugs and baskets Sardinia
specializes in these brightly coloured
handicrafts.

How much is it?
Quanto costa?

Great markets

Excellent places for souvenirs or just wandering around to absorb the local scene, Italy's street markets are quintessential elements of daily life. Among the most animated are:

Rialto, Venice Still redolent of its medieval origins, now mainly fruit and vegetables.

San Lorenzo, Florence Centred on the Mercato Centrale food market, but spreading out to encompass every other kind of article – especially good for leather goods.

Porta Portese, Rome A flea-market, jam-packed every Sunday morning.

Piazza Vittorio, Rome A much smaller market near Termini, good for fruit and vegetables, olives, cheeses and seafood.

La Forcella, Naples West of Piazza Garibaldi, this has the greatest concentration of stalls and back-street shops, selling everything from clucking chickens to mirror sunglasses.

Vucciria, Palermo A bustling, oriental-style market, where you can pick up anything from fried squid to penknives or a set of coffee cups.

Via Papireto, Palermo A flea-market and antiques exchange behind the Duomo.

Buying food

Most towns have open-air markets for the freshest produce. Prices are displayed and non-negotiable. Otherwise, for everyday items, you can find a range of foods at an *alimentari* (grocer's), including bread, cheeses and pasta. Most *alimentari* will also make up *panini* (rolls) for you. For delicacies and local specialities including salamis, find a *salumeria* (delicatessen). Super-markets are also found in every town.

Local Goods

Lace The Venetian island of Burano is the centre for lace and embroidered linen, though it's on sale throughout the Venice area. Orvieto in Umbria is also a small-scale centre for *merletto* (lace).

Glass Ubiquitous in Venice, though often gaudy and kitsch. Shop around and visit in particular the island of Murano.

Masks Carnival masks achieve a rare, often spooky, refinement in Venice, while those in Sardinia are equally eerie, but of a coarser, rustic style.

Jewellery Florence is a traditional centre for jewellers and goldsmiths.

Woodwork Orvieto is a major centre for wood-carved articles and veneers.

Ceramics Faenza, in Emilia-Romagna, famed for its 'faience' pottery; Deruta, in Umbria. For some of the splashiest designs, however, head south to Vietri sul Mare, on the Amalfi coast, or Santo Stefano di Camastra and Caltagirone in Sicily.
Coral Torre del Greco, south of Naples, and the west coast of Sardinia specialize in jewellery and ornaments made from coral.
Puppets Sicily is the home of puppet theatre, and some of the best puppets can be found in Palermo and Catania.

 I'm just looking, thank you.
Sto solo guardando.

Phrasemaker

Phrases to use anywhere

Do you have any (milk / stamps)?	**Ha (latte / francobolli)?**
How much is it?	**Quanto costa/viene?**
How much are they?	**Quanto costano/vengono?**
A . . . , please.	**Un/uno/una/un' . . . , per favore.**
This one, that one	**Questo/a, quello/a**
How much is it (altogether)?	**Quant'è (in tutto)?**
That's all, thank you.	**Basta così, grazie.**
Can I pay (with traveller's cheques / by credit card)?	**Posso pagare con (traveller's cheques / la carta di credito)?**

Prego?/Desidera?/Dica?	Can I help you?
No, mi dispiace.	I'm afraid not.
Quale?	Which one?
Ecco (a Lei).	Here you are.
Altro?	Anything else?
Allora, in tutto sono . . . euro.	Well, that's . . . euro altogether.

Shops

baker's	**il panificio / la panetteria / il forno**
bookshop	**la libreria**
butcher's	**la macelleria**
cake shop	**la pasticceria**
chemist	**la farmacia**
clothes shop	**il negozio di abbigliamento**
department store	**il grande magazzino**
florist	**il fioraio**
greengrocer's	**il fruttivendolo**
grocer's	**il negozio di alimentari**
hairdresser's	**la parrucchiera / il parrucchiere**
jeweller's	**la gioielleria**
newsagent's	**il giornalaio / l'edicola**
perfume shop	**la profumeria**
photography shop	**il fotografo**
shoe shop	**il negozio di scarpe**
stationery shop	**la cartoleria**

supermarket	**il supermercato**
tobacconist's	**il tabacchino / la tabaccheria**
toy shop	**il negozio di giocattoli**
travel agent's	**l'agenzia di viaggi**

Food shopping

How much (is it/are they) a kilo?	**Quanto costa/costano al chilo?**
A kilo of (apples / tomatoes)	**Un chilo di (mele / pomodori)**
Half a kilo of (cherries / grapes)	**Mezzo chilo di (ciliegie / uva)**
100 grammes of (parmesan / Parma ham)	**Un etto di (parmigiano / prosciutto crudo)**
(A bottle / packet) of . . .	**(Una bottiglia / un pacchetto) di**
A slice of . . .	**Una fetta di . . .**
Three slices of . . .	**Tre fette di . . .**
Can I try (some/a piece)?	**Posso assaggiare?**
A bit (more / less), please.	**Un po' di (più / meno), per favore.**

Quanto?   How much would you like?

packet	**il pacchetto**
sachet	**il sacchetto**
tin (of fish)	**la scatoletta (di pesce)**
tin (of tomatoes)	**il barattolo (di pomodori)**
tube	**il tubetto**

kilo	**un chilo**
half a kilo	**mezzo chilo**
100g	**un etto**
bag	**un sacchetto**
bottle	**la bottiglia**
can	**la lattina**
jar	**il vasetto**

Buying clothes or accessories

I'm just looking, thank you.	**Sto solo guardando, grazie.**
I'd like a (shirt / pair of trousers).	**Vorrei (una camicia / un paio di pantaloni).**
I'm size (14 [clothes] / 5 [shoes]).	**Ho (la taglia 42 / il numero 38).**
Can I try it on?	**Posso provarlo/la?**
Can I try them on?	**Posso provarli/le?**
It's a bit (big / small).	**È un po' (grande / piccolo/a).**
They're a bit (big / small).	**Sono un po' (grandi / piccoli/e).**
Do you have a smaller size?	**Ha (la taglia più piccola / il numero più piccolo)?**
Do you have anything cheaper?	**Ha qualcosa di più economico?**
Do you have the same in (yellow / black)?	**Ha lo stesso modello in (giallo / nero)?**
I like (it/them).	**Mi (piace/piacciono).**
I don't like (it/them).	**Non mi (piace/piacciono).**
I'll take it.	**Lo/la prendo.**
I'll take them.	**Li/le prendo.**
I'll think about it.	**Ci penso.**
*Can I have a discount?	**Mi fa uno sconto?**
(*worth asking at the market)	

Che (taglia/numero)?	What size [for clothes/for shoes]?
Di che colore?	What colour?
Il camerino è là in fondo.	The changing room is through there.
Come (va/vanno)?	How (does it/do they) fit?
Le (piace/piacciono)?	Do you like (it/them)?

61

Department store

Where is the (. . .) department?	**Dov'è il reparto (. . .)?**
Where can I find the biscuits?	**Dove sono i biscotti?**
Is there a lift?	**C'è l'ascensore?**

Al (pianterreno / primo piano / secondo piano / terzo piano)	On the (ground / first / second / third) floor* *(= first / second / third / fourth floor for US travellers)
Nel seminterrato	In the basement

Buying stamps

How much is a stamp for (Britain / the USA)?	**Quanto costa un francobollo per (la Gran Bretagna / gli Stati Uniti)?**
For a (letter / postcard)	**Da (lettera / cartolina)**
Four stamps, please.	**Quattro francobolli, per favore.**
A telephone card	**Una carta telefonica**
I'd like to send this to England.	**Vorrei spedire questo / a in Inghilterra.**

Photography

A 36 exposure film for (prints / slides)	**Un rullino di (foto / diapositive) da 36**
A packet of batteries	**Un pacchetto di pile**
Can you develop this film?	**Mi sviluppa questo rullino?**
When will it be ready?	**Quando è pronto?**

Oggi pomeriggio / Domani mattina	This afternoon / Tomorrow morning
Fra (un'ora / tre ore)	In (an hour / three hours)

Fruit

apples	**le mele**	oranges	**le arance**
apricots	**le albicocche**	peaches	**le pesche**
bananas	**le banane**	pears	**le pere**
cherries	**le ciliegie**	pineapple	**l'ananas**
figs	**i fichi**	plums	**le prugne**
grapes	**l'uva**	raspberries	**i lamponi**
lemons	**i limoni**	strawberries	**le fragole**
melon	**il melone**	watermelon	**il cocomero**

Vegetables

asparagus	**gli asparagi**	lettuce	**la lattuga**
aubergines	**le melanzane**	mushrooms	**i funghi**
basil	**il basilico**	onions	**le cipolle**
carrots	**le carote**	parsley	**il prezzemolo**
cauliflower	**il cavolfiore**	peas	**i piselli**
celery	**il sedano**	potatoes	**le patate**
cucumber	**il cetriolo**	spinach	**gli spinaci**
French beans	**i fagiolini**	tomatoes	**i pomodori**
garlic	**l'aglio**	artichokes	**i carciofi**
leeks	**i porri**		

Groceries

beer	**la birra**	lemonade	**la limonata**
biscuits	**i biscotti**	liqueurs	**i liquori**
butter	**il burro**	milk	**il (litro di) latte**
cheese	**il formaggio**	pepper	**il pepe**
coffee	**il caffè**	salt	**il sale**
crisps	**le patatine**	tea	**il tè**
eggs	**le uova**	washing-up	**il detersivo**
orange juice	**il succo di**	liquid	
	frutta	water	**l'acqua**
	all'arancia	(red / white)	**il vino (rosso /**
honey	**il miele**	wine	**bianco)**
jam /	**la marmellata**	yoghurt	**lo yogurt**
marmalade			

Bread
(for pastries, see Café life, p70)

baguette	**il filone**	white roll	**il panino**
ciabatta	**la ciabatta**	wholemeal roll	**il panino**
focaccia	**la focaccia**		**integrale**

Delicatessen

anchovies	**le acciughe**	mortadella	**la mortadella**
bacon	**la pancetta**	[US baloney]	
clams	**le vongole**	mussels	**le cozze**
ham	**il prosciutto**	salami	**il salame**
	cotto	sardines	**le sardine**
cured ham	**il prosciutto**	sausages	**le salsicce**
	crudo	tuna	**il tonno**

Toiletries

brush	**la spazzola**	soap	**il sapone**
comb	**il pettine**	tissues	**i fazzoletti di**
deodorant	**il deodorante**		**carta**
nappies	**i pannolini**	toilet paper	**la carta igienica**
sanitary towels	**gli assorbenti**	toothbrush	**lo spazzolino**
shampoo	**lo shampoo**	toothpaste	**il dentifricio**

Newsagent's/Tobacconist's

batteries	**le pile**	(English /	**il giornale**
cigarettes	**il pacchetto di**	American)	**(inglese /**
	sigarette	newspaper	**americano)**
envelope	**la busta**	pen	**la penna**
film	**il rullino**	postcard	**la cartolina**
guidebook	**la guida**	stamp	**il francobollo**
magazine	**la rivista**	sweets	**il pacchetto di**
map of the city	**la piantina**		**caramelle**
	della città	telephone card	**la carta tele-**
matches	**il pacchetto di**		**fonica**
	fiammiferi		

Souvenirs and local specialities

bracelet	**il braccialetto**	necklace	**la collana**
brooch	**la spilla**	painting	**il quadro**
camera	**la macchina fotografica**	plate	**il piatto**
		ring	**l'anello**
CD	**il CD**	tape	**la cassetta**
ceramics	**la ceramica**	vase	**il vaso**
earrings	**gli orecchini**	watch	**l'orologio**
frame	**la cornice**		

Clothes and accessories

bag	**la borsetta**	skirt	**la gonna**
belt	**la cintura**	socks	**i calzini**
bra	**il reggiseno**	sunglasses	**gli occhiali da sole**
coat	**il cappotto**		
gloves	**i guanti**	sweater	**il maglione**
hat	**il cappello**	swimming costume/trunks	**il costume da bagno**
jacket	**la giacca**		
raincoat	**l'impermeabile (m.)**	T-shirt	**la maglietta**
		tie	**la cravatta**
sandals	**i sandali**	tights	**il collant**
scarf	**la sciarpa**	tracksuit	**la tuta sportiva**
shirt/blouse	**la camicia**	trousers	**i pantaloni**
shoes	**le scarpe**	underpants	**le mutande**

Materials

corduroy	**il velluto a coste**	suede	**il camoscio**
		velvet	**il velluto**
cotton	**il cotone**	wool	**la lana**
denim	**il denim**	brass	**l'ottone (m.)**
lace	**il pizzo**	copper	**il rame**
leather	**il cuoio/la pelle**	glass	**il vetro**
linen	**il lino**	gold	**l'oro**
nylon	**il nailon**	plastic	**la plastica**
satin	**il raso**	silver	**l'argento**
silk	**la seta**	wood	**il legno**

Language works

Shopping at the market

1 Buying fruit and vegetables at the market
- ■ Dica.
- □ **Mezzo chilo di ciliegie e un chilo di pomodori, per favore.**
- ■ **5000 le ciliegie, 2800 i pomodori, altro?**
- □ Ha uva?
- ■ Sì, ecco.
- □ **Quanto costa al chilo?**
- ■ 4200.
- □ **Mezzo chilo, per favore.**
- ■ Altro?
- □ **Basta così, grazie. Quant'è?**

The most expensive item per kilo is . . .
Altogether you pay . . .

Buying clothes

2 You're looking for a pair of linen trousers
- ■ **Vorrei un paio di pantaloni di lino.**
- □ **Che taglia?**
- ■ 48.
- □ **Di che colore?**
- ■ **Nero. Quanto costano?**
- □ **83.000 lire.**
- ■ **Non mi piacciono in nero, ha lo stesso modello in blu?**
- □ **Sì, in blu, in bianco e in marrone, ecco.**
- ■ **Li prendo blu.**

What kind of trousers do you try on first?
What other colours are available?

3 Buying shoes at the market and getting a discount
- ■ **Scusi, quanto costano?**
- □ **Vengono 105.000. Che numero?**
- ■ 38.
- □ **Ecco. Come vanno?**
- ■ **Bene, ma . . . ha qualcosa di più economico o mi fa uno sconto?**
- □ **No no, mi dispiace.**
- ■ **Allora, . . . ci penso.**
- □ **Va bene allora, 95.000.**
- ■ **Le prendo.**

The shoes don't fit: true/false
You get a discount of 5000 lira: true/false

At the newsagent's

4 Stamps, a phone card and something to read
- ■ Prego?
- □ **Quanto costa un francobollo da cartolina per la Gran Bretagna?**
- ■ **750 lire.**
- □ **Due francobolli e una carta telefonica da 5000.**
- ■ Altro?
- □ **Prendo l'Economist.**
- ■ **Allora, in tutto sono 13.500.**

For the Economist you pay:
6500   7000   6000
Altogether you pay:
13.500   11.500   12.500

Try it out

Fill the gaps

Find the missing words from this list.
carta telefonica, orecchini, camicia, rullino, francobollo, pantaloni
1 una cartolina e un _____ per l'Inghilterra
2 un _____ per la macchina fotografica
3 una cintura per i _____
4 una cravatta per la _____
5 una _____ per telefonare
6 una collana e un paio di _____

Colours

Can you name all of these colours in Italian?
The colour of . . .
1 a stop light
2 grass
3 night
4 a dull day
5 milk
6 a canary

As if you were there

Use the English prompts to take part in the dialogue.
- (Point to a pair of glasses and ask how much they are.)
- □ **48.000.**
- (You like them, but has he got anything cheaper?)
- □ **Ecco a lei 25.000.**
- (A cheaper pair: but you don't like them . . .)
- □ **Gli occhiali da 48.000 sono firmati.**
- (He says they're designer glasses: ask for a discount)
- □ **Mi dispiace, 48.000.**
- (Say you'll think about it and thank him.)
- □ **Va bene, 45.000.**
- (Say you'll take them!)

Sound Check

g is pronounced differently depending on which vowel follows it
g + e or **i** like 'j' in 'jeans'
    gelato   jelato
    formaggio   formajo

g + a, o or **u** like 'g' in 'go'
    gamba   gamba
    gola   gola
    ragù   ragoo

g + h is also like 'g' in 'go'
    Inghilterra   eengilterra

Practise on these words:
buongiorno, gentile, ghiaccio, giallo, gola, ragazza

Café life

Cafés and bars are a very important part of the Italian lifestyle, frequented from early morning to late at night.

Bars are a good place to find breakfast; for Italians this is a solitary affair normally dispatched standing up at a bar, consisting of a *cappuccino* or *caffè espresso* with a *cornetto* (croissant). Bars are ubiquitous and varied, though the most common type is a chrome and mirrored affair with a Gaggia coffee machine. Bars where you can sit down are more common in Northern Italy; if you are served at the table, you are charged 50–100% more than if you stand at the bar.

> What sandwiches do you have?
> **Che tramezzini ha?**

An evening meal may be preceded by an aperitif at a sit-down bar, and followed by a coffee or ice-cream in a café, especially in summer. Don't forget to try out a *gelateria*, which serves only ice-creams to eat in or take away, and a *pasticceria*, a shop specializing in sweet pastries, often made on the premises.

> I'll have a cheese roll and a mineral water, please.
> **Vorrei un panino al formaggio e un'acqua minerale, per favore.**

Cafés and bars serve a wide variety of drinks, including alcohol, soft drinks and hot drinks. Most also serve food, usually sandwiches, rolls and pastries. There are no age restrictions. It is usual to leave a small tip on the table or in the saucer on the bar.

> Is there a toilet?
> **C'è una toilette?**

Phrasemaker

Asking what there is

Do you have any (sandwiches / grapefruit juice)?	**Ha (tramezzini / succo di frutta al pompelmo)?**
What (rolls / cakes) do you have?	**Che (panini / paste) ha?**
What soft drinks do you have?	**Che bibite ha?**

Prego?/Desidera?	What would you like?
Mi dispiace, è finito/a.	Sorry, we've run out of it.
Mi dispiace, sono finiti/e.	Sorry, we've run out of them.

Soft drinks

coke	**la coca-cola**
fruit juice	**il succo di frutta**
apricot	**all'albicocca**
grapefruit	**al pompelmo**
peach	**alla pesca**
pear	**alla pera**
freshly squeezed orange juice	**la spremuta d'arancia**
iced tea	**il tè freddo**
lemonade	**la limonata**
milkshake	**il frullato**

mineral water (still / fizzy)	**l'acqua minerale (naturale / gassata)**
orangeade	**l'aranciata**
tonic	**l'acqua tonica**
with a slice of lemon	**con una fetta di limone**
(with / without) ice	**(con / senza) ghiaccio**

Also look out for:
l'Aperol (a non-alcoholic aperitif)

Alcoholic drinks

beer	**la birra Moretti/Peroni/ Pedavena** (brands)
wine	**il vino**
white / red	**bianco / rosso**
brandy	**il cognac**
whisky	**il whisky**
gin (and tonic)	**il gin (tonico)**

Also look out for:
il Martini
il Cynar (an aperitif made from artichokes)
il Cinzano
il Campari (soda)
la grappa (an Italian brandy)
Asti spumante sparkling wine

Hot drinks

il caffè coffee
il caffè corretto coffee with a liqueur such as grappa /cognac
il caffelatte coffee with lots of hot milk
il caffè lungo weaker black coffee, served in a long glass
il cappuccino cappuccino
il macchiato coffee with just a little milk
il tè (al latte /al limone) tea with (milk / lemon)
la cioccolata calda hot chocolate
  (con / senza) panna (with / without) cream
  (con / senza) zucchero (with / without) sugar

Snacks

small pizza	**la pizzetta**	ham	**al prosciutto cotto**
slice of cheese pizza	**una fetta di pizza al formaggio**	Parma ham	**al prosciutto crudo**
roll (bread)	**il panino**	salami	**al salame**
sandwich	**il tramezzino**	with mushrooms	**ai funghi**
sandwich (toasted)	**il toast**	with tuna and tomatoes	**al tonno e pomodori**
bacon	**alla pancetta**		

Cakes

brioche	**la brioche**	pancake	**la frittella**
ring doughnut	**la ciambella**	without raisins	**senza uvetta**
cream croissant	**il cornetto alla crema**	doughnut	**il krapfen / bombolone**
croissant with jam	**il cornetto alla marmellata**		

Ice-creams

ice-cream	**il gelato**	lemon	**al limone**
banana	**alla banana**	bilberry	**ai mirtilli**
chocolate	**al cioccolato**	hazelnut	**alla nocciola**
coconut	**al cocco**	pistachio	**al pistacchio**
strawberry	**alla fragola**	chocolate chip	**alla stracciatella**
fruits of the forest	**ai frutti di bosco**	vanilla	**alla vaniglia**

Signs

Ordering

I'll have a (cheese roll / small pizza), please.	**Vorrei (un panino al formaggio / una pizzetta), per favore.**
I'll have a (white coffee / hot chocolate), please.	**Vorrei (un macchiato / una cioccolata calda), per favore.**
I'll have a (strawberry / lemon) ice-cream, please.	**Vorrei un gelato (alla fragola / al limone), per favore.**
This one / That one	**Questo/a / Quello/a**

Quale?	Which one?
Ecco a lei.	Here you are.
Con (panna / ghiaccio / limone)?	With (cream / ice / lemon)?
Qualcosa da bere?	Something to drink?
Gassata o naturale?	Fizzy or still?
In cono o coppetta?	Cone or bowl!?
Che gusto?	Which flavour (of ice-cream)?
Si serva pure.	It's self-service/Help yourself.
Deve fare lo scontrino alla cassa.	You need to get a receipt first at the till.

Containers

glass	**il bicchiere**		carafe	**la caraffa**
cone	**il cono**		bowl	**la coppetta**
jug	**il bricco**		tub	**la vaschetta**
pitcher	**la brocca**			

Other useful phrases

How much is it (altogether)?	**Quant'è (in tutto)?**
Is there a (toilet / telephone)?	**C'è (una toilette / un telefono)?**
Here you are.	**Ecco a lei.**

Ce n'è (una/uno) lì dietro.	There's one back there.
C'è un telefono a scatti.*	There's a private pay phone.

* (pay at the bar after the call)

Language works

Asking what there is

1 Sandwiches or rolls?
- **Ha tramezzini?**
- □ **Mi dispiace, solo panini: i tramezzini sono finiti.**
- **. . . Che panini ha?**
- □ **Al formaggio, al prosciutto, al salame . . .**
- **Un panino al formaggio e due birre.**
- □ **Ecco a lei. Allora il panino 2000 e le birre 7000. In tutto è . . .**

There are only rolls left: true/false
A beer costs 2500: true/false

Ordering

2 Ordering coffee and a cake for one
- **Prego?**
- □ **Un macchiato e una pasta, per favore.**
- **Quale? Questa?**
- □ **Quella, grazie. Quant'è?**
- **Allora, 1500 il caffè macchiato, e 1300 la pasta.**

Altogether you pay . . .

3 Ordering drinks and croissants for two
- **Un cappuccino, una cioccolata calda e due cornetti, per favore.**
- □ **La cioccolata con panna?**
- **No, senza.**
- □ **Per i cornetti si serva pure.**
- **Grazie. Quant'è?**
- □ **Allora, il cappuccino 2000, la cioccolata 2200, e i cornetti 2600. 6800 in tutto.**

A hot chocolate costs more than a croissant: true/false

4 Going for a snack
- **Vorrei un tramezzino ai funghi e due pizzette, per favore.**
- □ **Qualcosa da bere?**
- **. . . Un succo di frutta alla pera e un'acqua minerale.**
- □ **Gassata o naturale?**
- **Gassata e con ghiaccio e limone, per favore.**
- □ **Ecco a lei, ma mi dispiace il succo di frutta alla pera è finito.**
- **Ha succo di frutta al pompelmo?**
- □ **Sì.**
- **Grazie. Quant'è?**
- □ **Allora, 1600 il tramezzino, 5000 le pizzette, 1800 e 1500 le bibite.**

How much do you pay for the snacks?
Why can't you have pear juice and what do you order instead?

5 Stopping for a drink
- **Un tè al latte e un'aranciata, per favore.**
- □ **Prima deve fare lo scontrino alla cassa.**
- **Va bene.**
(You go to the till)
- **Un tè al latte e un'aranciata, per favore.**
- □ **2300 il tè e 1800 l'aranciata.**
- **Scusi c'è una toilette?**
- □ **Sì, ce n'è una lì dietro.**

You have to pay at the till before you order: true/false
Altogether you pay 4100: true/false
There's no toilet: true/false

6 Going for an ice-cream
- **Tre gelati da 2000 e uno da 3000, per favore.**
- □ **In cono o in coppetta?**
- **In cono.**
- □ **Che gusto?**
- **Due al limone e due alla stracciatella e nocciola.**

You pay with a 10.000 lire note: how much change do you get?

Try it out

Split words

Put together the parts of words below to find five flavours of ice-cream.
CRE: FRA: STAC: CIO: CO: LA: NOC: PI: MA: LA: CHIO: COC: GO

Fill the gaps

Complete the missing words: we've given you one of the letters to get you started!

Un cornetto alla _ A _ _ _ _ _A_A
Una frittella senza _ _ _ _ _A
Una cioccolata con _ A _ _ A
Un caffè _ A _ _ _ _ A _ _
Un tè al _ A _ _ _

Questions & answers

Can you match each question to its answer?
1 **Scusi, c'è un telefono?**
   a **Una brioche, per favore.**
2 **Quale?**
   b **2350.**
3 **Che gusto?**
   c **Sì, un Martini, per favore.**
4 **Prego?**
   d **Ce n'è uno a scatti.**
5 **Quant'è?**
   e **Questa.**
6 **Qualcosa da bere?**
   f **Stracciatella.**

As if you were there

Can you reconstruct the following conversation?
☐ **3500.**
■ **Alla crema.**
☐ **Sì, ce n'è una lì dietro.**
■ **Un caffellatte e un cornetto.**
☐ **Prego?**
■ **Scusi, c'è una toilette?**
☐ **Alla crema o alla marmellata?**
■ **Grazie.**

Sound Check

The pronunciation of **s** changes depending on the letters around it.

s between two vowels, like 's' in 'rose'
   naso   nazo
   casa   caza
s + anything else, like 's' in 'state'
   estate   estate

Practise on these words:
borsa, chiuso, costa, pista, riso, scusi

Eating out

Meals

Lunch takes place between noon and 2 pm, and varies from a *tramezzino* (sandwich) or *panino* (roll) to a full-blown meal in a *trattoria* or restaurant. Dining out at night (about 8–11 pm) may take place in a *trattoria*, a more formal restaurant, or an informal *pizzeria*. Note that a cover charge (*coperto*) per person will be added to the bill wherever you sit down to eat.

❗ What do you recommend?
Che cosa consiglia?

Where to eat

Tavola calda Offers fast-food Italian-style: pre-cooked pastas, pizzas and meat dishes, with wine, beer or soft drinks to wash it down.

Pizzeria Has pizzas and beers and occasionally a restaurant menu as well. The best pizzerias have wood-fired ovens (*forno a legna*).

Trattoria An informal, often family-run establishment with a short list of dishes and local wine in carafes. Not all *trattorie* will have a written menu with prices. Ask the waiter for recommendations.

Osteria Ranging from a down-to-earth tavern with a small menu to a chic, old-world type restaurant specializing in country fare, though often at inflated prices.

Ristorante A formal dining-place with a more extensive menu and smarter service. They will generally be more expensive.

❗ What's the local speciality?
Qual è la specialità locale?

Types of food

The type of food on offer in an Italian restaurant will vary enormously according to the region. Pasta is popular everywhere. *Polenta* is a favourite starter in Northern Italy and couscous features in western Sicily, where North African influence is strongest. Lamb and veal are regularly on menus, but you will also find rabbit, game and wild boar in Umbria, pork as a staple in the Veneto and Calabria, and horsemeat a delicacy in Sardinia. Fish and seafood are available throughout Italy, though with seasonal variations: restaurants are required to specify if it is frozen (*surgelato*). As for vegetables and fruit, pick whatever's in season and you can't go far wrong.

❗ I'd like the set menu, please.
Vorrei il menù (a prezzo fisso), per favore.

Italy is a good place for vegetarians, with the wide availability of pasta and vegetable sauces. Some sauces and stocks, however, may contain meat stock: check with the waiter, if in doubt.

❗ Does it contain meat stock?
C'é brodo di carne?
The bill, please.
Mi porta il conto, per favore?

Phrasemaker

Finding somewhere to eat

Is there a good restaurant near here?
C'è un buon ristorante qui vicino?

At the restaurant

ashtray	**il portacenere**
bottle	**la bottiglia**
bowl (dessert)	**la coppetta**
bowl (soup)	**il piatto fondo**
chair	**la sedia**
coffee cup	**la tazzina**
fork	**la forchetta**
glass	**il bicchiere**
knife	**il coltello**
napkin	**il tovagliolo**
oil	**l'olio**
pepper	**il pepe**
plate	**il piatto**
salt	**il sale**
saucer	**il piattino**
spoon	**il cucchiaio**
table	**la tavola**
tablecloth	**la tovaglia**
teaspoon	**il cucchiaino**
toothpicks	**gli stuzzica-denti**
vinegar	**l'aceto**

Arriving

A table for (two / four), please.
Un tavolo per (due / quattro), per favore.

I have a reservation for . . .
Ho prenotato per . . .

Asking about the menu

I'd like the (set) menu, please.
Vorrei il menù (a prezzo fisso), per favore.

What is . . .?
Che cos'è . . .?

What do you recommend?
Che cosa consiglia?

What's the local speciality?
Qual è la specialità locale?

Have you got . . . ?
Ha . . .?

Is (bread / the cover charge) included?
È incluso il (pane / coperto)?

Ordering

I'll have . . .	**Prendo . . .**
To drink . . .	**Da bere . . .**
A (bottle / carafe) of . . .	**Una (bottiglia / caraffa) di . . .**
Half a bottle of. . .	**Mezza bottiglia di . . .**
As a (starter / first course / second course / side dish / dessert) . . .	**Come (antipasto / primo / secondo / contorno / dessert) . . .**
No starter for me.	**Niente antipasto per me.**

Pronti per ordinare?	Are you ready to order?
(Non) è incluso.	It's (not) included.
Si paga a parte.	It's extra.
Oggi abbiamo . . .	Today we have . . .
(Che) cosa prende/prendono?	What would you like?
Mi dispiace è finito/a . . .	Sorry, we're out of . . .
Come (la/lo) vuole?	How would you like it done?
Vuole il dessert?	Would you like a dessert?
Buon appetito!	Enjoy your meal!

Eating preferences

I'm allergic to (onion / seafood / garlic).	**Sono allergico/a (alla cipolla / ai frutti di mare / all'aglio).**
I'm vegetarian.	**Sono vegetariano/a.**
I'm vegan.	**Non mangio latticini.**
Does it contain . . . ?	**C'è . . .?**

During the meal

Excuse me! / Waiter!	**Scusi! / Cameriere!**
I didn't order any . . .	**Non ho ordinato . . .**
More bread, please.	**Mi porta ancora un po' di pane, per favore?**
Another bottle of . . .	**Un'altra bottiglia di . . .**
It's (delicious / very good).	**È (squisito / molto buono).**
It's (cold / raw / burnt).	**È (freddo / crudo / bruciato).**
Where are the toilets?	**Dove sono le toilette?**

Per chi è il risotto?	Who is the risotto for?
Tutto bene?	Is everything all right?
Altro?	Anything else?

Paying

The bill, please.	**Mi porta il conto, per favore?**
Do you take credit cards?	**Accettate carte di credito?**
There is a mistake, I think.	**C'è un errore, credo.**
We didn't have any beer.	**Non abbiamo preso birra.**
Is service included?	**È incluso il servizio?**

Menus

Menù a prezzo fisso	Set price menu
Pane, grissini e coperto	Bread and cover charge
Servizio incluso	Service included
Piatto del giorno	Dish of the day
Piatti freddi	Cold dishes

Regional specialities

Emilia-Romagna: prosciutto, parmigiano, tortellini; wine – Lambrusco

Lazio: gnocchi, saltimbocca alla romana, pecorino; wine – Frascati

Liguria: lasagne/trenette al pesto

Lombardy: risotto alla milanese, costoletta alla milanese, gorgonzola, osso buco; wines – Barolo, Barbera

Naples: spaghetti alle vongole, pizza margherita

Sicily: arancini, pescespada, cassata siciliana; wine – Marsala

Tuscany: bruschetta, triglie alla livornese, bistecca alla fiorentina, cinghiale, panforte; wine – Chianti

Umbria: porcini and tartufo

Venice: risi e bisi, fegato alla veneziana, baccalà, asiago, zuppa di cozze, risotto alle seppie; wines – Merlot, Tocai, Bardolino, Valpolicella

Other specialities

Christmas: panettone – a large sweet bread with raisins and candied lemon peel; pandoro – a large sponge cake

Easter: la colomba – a dove-shaped cake similar to a panettone with almonds on the top

Carnival: frittelle – small cakes with raisins and custard filling; galani o chiacchiere – small pastries covered in sugar

Language works

Asking about the menu

1 Choosing a menu and something to drink
- ■ Vorrei il menù a prezzo fisso.
- □ Ecco a lei. Da bere cosa prendono?
- ■ Da bere, una birra Moretti e una coca-cola, per favore.
- □ Ecco.
- ■ Grazie . . . Scusi, è incluso il pane?
- □ No, si paga a parte.

The bread is not included in the price: true/false

Ordering

2 Going for a pizza with a friend
- ■ Una pizza ai funghi . . . e che cos'è 'calzone'?
- □ Una pizza farcita con uova, ricotta, spinaci e cipolla.
- ■ Sono allergico alla cipolla.
- □ Vuole un calzone senza cipolla?

What's in the calzone?

3 Going for a meal on your last evening in Italy
- ■ Buonasera. Ho prenotato per due, Florio.
- □ Sì, da questa parte, prego. Ecco il menù.
  . . .
- □ Pronti per ordinare?
- ■ Sì, grazie, da bere una bottiglia di acqua minerale gassata e una bottiglia di vino bianco. Ha Orvieto?
- □ Sì.

What do you get to drink?

4 Ordering food
- □ Che cosa prendono come primo?
- ■ Qual è la specialità locale?
- □ Risi e bisi come primo e fegato alla veneziana come secondo.
- ■ Allora, due risi e bisi come primo e un fegato alla veneziana e un pollo arrosto come secondo.

What are the local specialities?

Try it out

Ordering food

Use the prompts (in the right sequence) to order your meal. Don't forget to ask for the bill!

a truffle-shaped ice-cream
grilled trout
ham and melon
seafood risotto
French beans
the bill
a bottle of red wine
chocolate cake

Crossword

Across
4 Mi porta un altro ____, per favore?
5 La carne è ____.
6 È incluso il ____?
8 La pizza è ____.

Down
1 Gli spaghetti sono ____.
2 Il risotto è ____.
3 Mi dispiace, gli spinaci sono ____.
7 Sono allergico alla ____.

The right dish for the right person

Work out from what each person says exactly what they ordered.
1 risotto di pesce
2 spaghetti alle vongole
3 una pizza margherita
4 una pizza capricciosa

Roberta – Sono allergica al pesce.
Carla – Sono vegetariana.
Giulio – Vorrei un piatto di pasta.
Franco — Scusi, c'è un errore, io non ho ordinato pizza.

Sound Check

Note the unusual pronunciations of the combinations **gl** and **gn**.

gl like 'lli' in 'million'
   bottiglia   botteelya

gn like 'ny' in 'canyon'
   gnocchi   nyokkee
   ogni   onyee

Practise on these words: **agnello, famiglia, gli, insegnare, luglio**

Menu reader

Courses

Antipasto – Starter
Starters usually include cold meats, and seafood and vegetable dishes; often a selection of starters will be brought to your table (*antipasti assortiti*), giving you the chance to sample a wide range. Look out for *antipasto misto* (a selection of cold meats), *melanzane* (aubergines) and *calamari* (squid).

Primo – First main dish
This will either be pasta in one of its diverse forms or a rice dish, *risotto*. The classic spaghetti dish is *spaghetti al ragù* and filled pastas, such as *tortellini* and *ravioli*, are also excellent. Look out for *risotto ai funghi* (with mushrooms) and *risotto alla marinara* (with seafood). In Northern Italy, polenta is a popular alternative: this is a kind of maize, which is boiled and then often fried and served with a sauce.

Secondo – Second main dish
Meat (*carne*) or fish (*pesce*), with a side-dish of salad or vegetables. Meat dishes not to be missed include *bistecca alla fiorentina* and *saltimbocca alla romana*. Note that fish is usually priced by weight: *tonno* (tuna) and *pescespada* (swordfish) are good.

Contorno – side-dish
Either a salad (eg *un' insalata mista* – mixed salad – or *un' insalata verde* – green salad) or vegetables (*verdura*), such as *spinaci* (spinach), *patate* (potatoes) or *zucchini* (courgettes).

Formaggio – cheese
Cheese is not generally served as a separate course in Italy, but you will come across Italian cheeses in other dishes, in particular the ubiquitous parmesan (as well as pecorino, which is similar, but made from sheep's milk), mozzarella and, in both savoury and sweet dishes, mascarpone and ricotta. The blue cheese gorgonzola is well worth trying.

Dessert (also often called *dolce*)
Either fruit, including *macedonia* (fruit salad), or a sweet such as *gelato* (ice-cream), a *torta*, eg *torta al cioccolato* (chocolate cake) or a *tiramisù*.

Main ways of cooking

arrosto	roasted	**alla griglia**	grilled
bollito/lesso	boiled	**ripieno/farcito**	stuffed
alla brace	grilled	**allo spiedo**	on the spit
cotto a vapore	steamed	**in umido**	stewed
ai ferri	grilled/bar-becued		
al forno	baked	**al sangue**	rare
fritto	fried	**a puntino**	medium
		ben cotto	well-done

The menu

abbacchio roast lamb
acciughe anchovies
aglio garlic
agnello lamb
agro with a lemon juice and oil dressing
albicocca apricot
alici anchovies
ananas pineapple
anatra all'arancia duck in orange sauce
antipasto misto selection of cold meats, including ham and salami

aragosta lobster
arancia orange
arancini (bianchi / rossi) rice balls with (cheese / meat) filling
asiago fresh mild cheese
asparagi asparagus
baccalà salt cod
bagna cauda hot anchovy and garlic dip, served with raw vegetables
banana banana
basilico basil
Bel Paese a creamy cheese
bistecca grilled steak
  alla fiorentina with pepper, lemon juice and parsley
bollito misto mixed boiled meat (mostly Northern Italy)
broccoli broccoli

81

bruschetta

riccio

bruschetta slices of toasted bread spread with a combination of tomatoes, oregano, mushrooms and oil
budino cold custard/chocolate dessert
burro butter
calamari squid
calzone pizza rolled up and filled
cannelloni pasta tubes
caponata a Southern Italian salad made with olives, anchovies and aubergines
carciofi artichokes
carne meat
carote carrots
cassata ice-cream made with ricotta and candied fruit
cassata siciliana sponge cake with candied fruit
cavolfiore cauliflower
cavolo cabbage
ceci chickpeas
cetriolo cucumber
ciliegie cherries
cinghiale wild boar
cioccolato chocolate
cipolle onions
cocomero watermelon
coniglio rabbit
costoletta veal cutlet
  alla milanese in breadcrumbs
cozze mussels
crostata di mele apple tart

crostini toast, croutons
dolce dessert or sweet
dolcelatte a soft cheese
fagioli haricot or butter beans
fagiolini French beans
farfalle pasta in small butterfly shapes
faraona guinea fowl
fegato liver
  alla veneziana fried with onions
fettucine ribbon pasta
fichi figs
finocchio fennel
formaggio cheese
fragole strawberries
frittata omelette
  ai funghi mushroom omelette
  al prosciutto ham omelette
fritto misto (di mare) assorted fried fish and seafood
frutta fresca (di stagione) fresh fruit (in season)
frutti di mare seafood
funghi mushrooms
  porcini cep mushrooms
gamberi prawns
gamberetti shrimps
gelato ice-cream
gnocchi little dumplings
gorgonzola a blue cheese

granchio crab
insalata salad
  caprese tomato and mozzarella salad with oregano and olive oil
  mista mixed
  di pomodori tomato
  verde green
involtini slices of meat rolled and stuffed with ham/bacon and sage
lamponi raspberries
lasagne lasagne (pasta sheets)
lattuga lettuce
lenticchie lentils
limone lemon
linguine flat spaghetti
maccheroni macaroni
macedonia fruit salad
maiale pork
mandorle almonds
manzo beef

mascarpone a rich cream cheese
mela apple
melanzane aubergines
melone melon
merluzzo cod
miele honey
minestra soup
  in brodo small pasta shapes in broth or stock
minestrone minestrone, thick vegetable soup
more blackberries
mortadella mild spiced salami
mozzarella a creamy cheese used in savoury and sweet dishes
nocciola hazelnut
noci walnuts
olio oil

mozzarella

manzo carpaccio

olio

osso buco with polenta

parmigiano

olive olives
osso buco veal/beef knuckles cooked in wine and lemon
ostriche oysters
pagliata sweetbreads
panettone a large sweet bread with raisins and candied lemon peel
panforte a dense cake with dried and candied fruits
panna cream

parmigiano parmesan
pasta e fagioli soup with noodles and beans
patate potatoes
patatine fritte chips
pecorino cheese made from sheep's milk
penne tube-shaped pasta
peperonata mixed sweet peppers

pasta

panettone

pera pear
pesca peach
pesce fish
pescespada swordfish
piselli peas
polenta a kind of maize, which is
boiled and then often fried
pollo chicken
   alla diavola arrosto very spicy
   grilled chicken
   petti di pollo chicken breast
polpo octopus
pomodoro tomato
pompelmo grapefruit
porcini wild cep mushrooms
porri leeks
prezzemolo parsley
prosciutto ham
   affumicato smoked
   crudo cured
   cotto cooked
prugne plums
radicchio dark red, slightly bitter
lettuce
rape turnip-tops
ravioli small square-shaped
pasta containing a filling
riccio sea urchin
ricotta a creamy soft cheese
rigatoni ribbed tubes of pasta
riso rice
   risi e bisi rice with peas and
   bacon

risotto

risotto a rice dish
   alla milanese with saffron and
   white wine
   di pesce with fish
   alla marinara with seafood
rognoni kidneys
rombo turbot
salame salami
salmone salmon
salsicce spicy sausages
saltimbocca alla romana veal
escalope in marsala with ham
and sage
salvia sage
scaloppine small slices of veal
sedano celery
sgombro mackerel
sogliola sole

porcini

carne

85

spaghetti

spaghetti spaghetti (long, thin pasta)
spezzatino a kind of stew
spigola sea bass
spinaci spinach
sugo sauce
tacchino turkey
tagliatelle ribbon pasta
tartufi truffles
tartufo truffle-shaped vanilla/chocolate ice-cream
tiramisù sponge soaked in coffee and alcohol with a mascarpone cream
tonno tuna
torta cake
  al cioccolato chocolate
  di mandorle almond

tortellini small filled pasta shapes
triglia red mullet
trippa tripe
trota trout
uova eggs
uva grapes
vaniglia vanilla
verdura (mista) (mixed) vegetables
vitello veal
vongole clams
zampone stuffed pig's trotter
zucchini courgettes
zuppa soup
  di pesce fish
  inglese kind of trifle

Main sauces

aglio, olio e peperoncino garlic, olive oil and chilli / spicy pepper

all'amatriciana tomatoes, red peppers, bacon, onion, garlic, white wine

all'arrabbiata tomatoes, chilli, herbs

al burro butter, grated parmesan

alla cacciatora onions, tomatoes, mushrooms, peppers, wine

alla carbonara bacon, onion, eggs, cheese

al pesto pine kernels, basil, garlic, cheese, marjoram

alla pizzaiola tomatoes, garlic, basil

ai quattro formaggi with four different cheeses

al ragù tomatoes, minced meat, onions, herbs

al sugo tomatoes

alle vongole clams, tomatoes, garlic, herbs

formaggi

Drinks

acqua water
  minerale mineral water
  del rubinetto tap water
  tonica tonic water
Acquavite type of liqueur, like brandy
Amaretto an almond liqueur
Aperol a non-alcoholic aperitif
aranciata orangeade, fizzy orange
birra beer
  alla spina draught
  estera imported
caffè coffee
  caffè corretto coffee with a liqueur such as grappa/cognac
  caffellatte coffee with lots of hot milk
  caffè lungo weaker black coffee, served in a long glass
  cappuccino cappuccino
  macchiato coffee with just a little milk
cioccolata hot chocolate
cognac brandy
Cynar an aperitif made from artichokes
frullato milk shake

gassato/a sparkling, fizzy
gin (tonico) gin and tonic
grappa liqueur made from grape must
latte milk
limonata lemonade
Marsala a Sicilian dessert wine
non gassato/a still
Sambuca an aniseed liqueur
spremuta fresh fruit juice
  d'arancia orange
  di limone lemon
spumante sparkling wine
succo di frutta fruit juice
  all'albicocca apricot
  al pompelmo grapefruit
  alla pesca peach
  alla pera pear
tè tea
  al latte with milk
  freddo iced
vino wine
  bianco white
  dolce sweet
  rosso red
  secco dry
whisky whisky

Italian wines

red **Merlot, Chianti, Barolo, Bardolino, Valpolicella, Lambrusco, Barbera, Montepulciano**

white **Frascati, Soave, Orvieto**
sparkling **Asti spumante**
dessert wine **Vin Santo, Marsala**

Italian beers

Moretti, Peroni, Pedavena

Pizzas

Pizza margherita cheese, tomatoes, oregano
Pizza ai funghi cheese, mushrooms, ham
Pizza capricciosa ham, mushrooms, pickled artichokes, olives
Pizza quattro stagioni assorted vegetables plus ham, cheese, tomatoes

Pizza vegetariana assorted vegetables, cheese, tomatoes
Calzone a 'folded-over' pizza, with different fillings
Pizza al taglio pizza sold in slices
Pizza da asporto take-away pizza

Entertainment and leisure

Finding out what's on

What is there to see here?
Che cosa c'è da vedere qui?

■ Italian newspapers: most of the national dailies – *Il Corriere della Sera*, *Il Messaggero* and *La Repubblica*, and in the south, *Il Giornale di Sicilia* and *La Gazzetta del Sud* – have local editions listing cultural events in the cities.

■ Local tourist offices: your first stop for information on concerts, films, plays and festivals. In the larger towns, they can provide English-language booklets (updated weekly or monthly) giving comprehensive tourist information.

■ English-language newspapers: in Rome, the fortnightly *Wanted in Rome* has some listings, while the weekly 'what's on', *Roma C'è*, has pages in English.

Spectator events

Sports
Football, motor-racing and cycling are the sports closest to Italian hearts.

Football Not so much a national sport, rather an obsession. Go to a match in any of the big cities to experience crowd participation and pre- and post-match festivities. The season runs from about September to June. Enquire from the local tourist offices where to buy tickets.

Motor racing The biggest fixtures are the Grand Prix at Monza, near Milan (September), and San Marino's Grand Prix at Imola (May).

Cycling The Giro d'Italia (May) excites the same kind of passion as the Tour de France.

Fairs and Festivals
Every village has at least one *festa* during the year, usually celebrating a saint's day, while the festivities in towns such as Venice and Siena are huge boisterous affairs. Find out from tourist offices about local events, and see Holidays, p24.

Do you have a map of the town?
Ha una pianta della città?

Music

Italians place a high value on music and you should try to experience concerts and recitals in atmospheric settings – in churches or outdoors, for example in Verona's Roman amphitheatre or Taormina's Greek theatre. The Umbria Jazz Festival is the best-known non-classical event (see Holidays). For a full-blown opera performance, visit La Scala, Milan and the Teatro San Carlo, Naples.

Cinema

Italian cinema is world-renowned, though it is Hollywood which dominates local screens. Foreign films are nearly always dubbed, but there are English-language cinemas in Milan and Rome. The Venice Film Festival is an important date in any film buff's calendar (see Holidays).

Is there a guided tour?
C'è una visita guidata?

Participation events

Swimming Beaches, most crowded in August, are relatively empty in June and September. Pollution is a continuing problem, especially around major river outlets: check first before taking the plunge. Many hotels have their own swimming pools.

Walking Unspoilt coastline and mountains offer endless opportunities for keen walkers. Nature reserves and national parks have some of the best hiking terrain.

Skiing There are accessible slopes throughout the peninsula: the Alps (from Milan, Turin and Venice); the Abruzzo (from Rome); the Sila and Aspromonte in Calabria and Mount Etna and the Monti Madonie in Sicily. The season runs December – March.

Tennis The larger hotels have facilities; otherwise ask at the local tourist office for details of public courts.

Cycling and horse-riding Bicycle-hire has become much easier in recent years, with rental shops in most large towns. The hills of

Tuscany and Umbria and the flatlands around the Po delta are popular for cycling. Pony hire is relatively difficult to arrange: again, Tuscany and Umbria offer most possibilities. Ponies are sometimes available as part of an *agriturismo* scheme (see p47). Ask at the tourist office for details.

Windsurfing and water-skiing You will still find water-ski facilities in most large beach resorts, but windsurfing is more popular: short courses and equipment rental are easy to come by.

Scuba diving You can enrol for crash-courses in diving at some resorts, especially off rocky coasts where the water is clear, for example the islands around Sicily.

Children

Children are worshipped in Italy and widely welcomed. Cities, however, are not child-friendly, unless you visit older centres where cars are restricted. Some cities have a funfair (*luna park*), but kids will probably have most fun just playing on the beach. Most hotels will offer a baby-sitting service, though it is quite common to see young children in restaurants until late.

Can you recommend a restaurant?
Mi può consigliare un buon ristorante?

Phrasemaker

Getting to know the place

Do you have (a map of the town / an entertainment guide)?	**Ha (una pianta della città / un programma degli spettacoli)?**
Do you have any information in English?	**Ha informazioni in inglese, per favore?**
What is there to see here?	**Che cosa c'è da vedere qui?**
What is there to do here (for the children)?	**Che cosa c'è da fare qui (per i bambini)?**
Is there a (guided tour / bus tour)?	**C'è (una visita guidata / un giro turistico)?**
Is there a football match on (today / Saturday)?	**C'è una partita di calcio (oggi / sabato)?**
Are there any (cinemas / night-clubs)?	**Ci sono (cinema / night-club)?**
Can you recommend a restaurant?	**Mi può consigliare un buon ristorante?**

C'è una visita guidata.	There's a guided tour.
Ci sono (le grotte / due teatri).	There are (the caves / two theatres).
Che cosa le interessa?	What are you interested in?

Things to do or see

English	Italian	English	Italian
cinema	**il cinema**	minigolf	**il minigolf**
concert	**il concerto**	museum	**il museo**
dance hall	**la sala da ballo**	night-club	**il night-club**
disco	**la discoteca**	opera	**l'opera lirica**
exhibition	**la mostra**	show	**lo spettacolo**
festival	**la festa**	stadium	**lo stadio**
fireworks	**i fuochi d'artificio**	swimming pool	**la piscina**
football match	**la partita di calcio**	tennis courts	**i campi da tennis**
funfair	**il luna park**	tennis match	**la partita di tennis**
gallery	**la galleria**	theatre	**il teatro**
golf course	**il corso di golf**		

Getting more information

Where is the (swimming pool / concert hall)?	Dov'è la (piscina / sala concerti)?
What time does the guided tour (start / finish)?	A che ora (comincia / finisce) la visita guidata?
What events are on this week?	Che spettacoli ci sono questa settimana?
When is it open?	Quando è aperto/a?
Do you need tickets?	Ci vuole il biglietto?
Are there any tickets?	Ci sono biglietti?
Where do you buy tickets?	Dove si comprano i biglietti?

Non serve il biglietto.	You don't need tickets.
Mi dispiace, è tutto esaurito.	Sorry, it's sold out.
Nella piazza principale alle dieci	In the main square at 10 o'clock
Dalle nove e mezza del mattino alle sette di sera	From 9.30 am to 7 pm
Alla biglietteria	At the ticket office
Qui sulla (mappa / pianta)	Here on the (map / plan)

Signs

Poltrona	Stall in a theatre	**Scale**	Stairs
Platea	Stall in a cinema	**Entrata**	Way in
		Uscita	Exit
Galleria	Balcony/circle	**Toilette**	Toilets
Palco	box	**Donne**	Ladies
Guardaroba	Cloakroom	**Uomini**	Gents

Entertainments

guide book	**la guida**	theatre box office	**il botteghino**
matinée	**lo spettacolo del pomeriggio**	ticket	**il biglietto**
		ticket office	**la biglietteria**
programme	**il programma**	in the original language	**in lingua originale**
seat in the circle	**il posto in galleria**		

Getting in

Do you have any tickets?	**Ha biglietti?**
How much (is it / are they)?	**Quanto costa/costano?**
Two tickets, please	**Due biglietti, per favore**
for (Saturday / tomorrow)	**per (sabato / domani)**
Are there any concessions?	**Ci sono riduzioni?**
How long does it last?	**Quanto dura?**
Does the film have subtitles?	**Il film ha i sottotitoli?**
Do you have the programme?	**Ha il programma?**
Is there an interval?	**C'è un intervallo?**
Are the seats numbered?	**I posti sono numerati?**
Is this place free?	**È libero questo posto?**

Sì, per (studenti / bambini / pensionati)	Yes, for (students / children / pensioners)
C'è un intervallo di venti minuti.	There's an interval of 20 minutes.
È (libero / occupato).	It's (free / taken).

Swimming and sunbathing

Can I use the hotel pool?	**Posso usare la piscina dell'albergo?**
Where are the (changing rooms / showers)?	**Dove sono le (cabine / docce)?**
I'd like to hire a (parasol / deck-chair).	**Vorrei noleggiare (un ombrellone / una sdraia).**

On the beach

boat	**la barca**
changing room (on the beach)	**la cabina**
deck-chair	**la sdraia**
life-guard	**il bagnino**
life-ring	**il salvagente**
sunbed	**il lettino**
sunglasses	**gli occhiali da sole**
suntan cream	**la crema solare**
towel	**l'asciugamano**
umbrella/sunshade	**l'ombrellone (m.)**

Sports

Where can I (go swimming / play tennis)?

Dove posso (nuotare / giocare a tennis)?

I'd like to hire (a racket / waterskis).

Vorrei noleggiare (una racchetta / degli sci nautici).

I'd like to take (skiing / sailing) lessons.

Vorrei prendere lezioni di (sci / vela).

Le lezioni (individuali / di gruppo) costano . . .

(Individual / Group) lessons cost . . .

climbing	l'alpinismo	skiing	lo sci
cycling	il ciclismo	surfing	il surf
football	il calcio	tennis	il tennis
golf	il golf	volleyball	la pallavolo
riding	l'equitazione	walking	la marcia
sailing	la vela	waterski	lo sci nautico

Sports equipment

boots	gli scarponi
dinghy	il canotto
gloves	i guanti
golf club	la mazza da golf
sailing boat	la barca a vela
salopettes	la tuta da sci
skates	i pattini
skating rink	la pista di pattinaggio
ski lift	la sciovia
ski run	la pista da sci
for (beginners / intermediate / advanced skiers)	per (principianti / sciatori intermedi / sciatori avanzati)
skis	gli sci
surfboard	la tavoletta da surf
tennis ball	la pallina
tennis racket	la racchetta
water skis	gli sci nautici

Language works

Getting to know the place

1 At tourist information
- ■ **Buongiorno, ha una pianta della città?**
- □ **Ecco a lei.**
- ■ **. . . Che cosa c'è da vedere qui?**
- □ **C'è la Rocca Scaligera e ci sono le grotte di Catullo.**
- ■ **. . . Ha informazioni in inglese?**
- □ **Ecco a lei. C'è una visita guidata della città domani alle dieci.**
- ■ **Grazie.**

There are two main sites to visit: true/false
What starts at ten o'clock tomorrow?

2 Trying to keep everybody happy
- ■ **Scusi, cosa c'è da fare qui per i bambini?**
- □ **C'è il tennis, il minigolf, c'è il luna park e ci sono i fuochi d'artificio domani.**
- ■ **Ci sono cinema?**
- □ **C'è il cinema Rossini.**
- ■ **Ha il programma degli spettacoli?**
- □ **Ecco a lei.**

What activities and entertainment are there for children?
What are you given?

Getting more information

3 Going to a concert
- ■ **Scusi, dov'è la sala concerti?**
- □ **Nella piazza principale.**
- ■ **Ci vuole il biglietto per il concerto?**
- □ **No, non serve il biglietto.**
- ■ **A che ora finisce?**
- □ **Alle 10.50.**

Where is the concert hall?
Do you need tickets?

Getting in

4 Going on a guided tour
- ■ **Buongiorno, a che ora comincia la visita guidata?**
- □ **Alle 11.**
- ■ **Quanto dura?**
- □ **Un'ora.**
- ■ **Quanto costa?**
- □ **10.000.**
- ■ **Ci sono riduzioni?**
- □ **5000 per i bambini.**
- ■ **2 adulti e 2 bambini, per favore.**

When does the tour finish?
How much do you pay?

5 Going to the opera
- ■ **Ha biglietti per domani?**
- □ **Mi dispiace, domani è tutto esaurito. Ci sono biglietti per sabato pomeriggio.**
- ■ **Va bene. Due posti in galleria, per favore.**
- □ **15a e 15b. 55.000, prego.**
- ■ **Grazie. Ha un programma?**
- □ **Ecco a lei, 5500.**
- ■ **Quanto dura lo spettacolo?**
- □ **Tre ore.**
- ■ **C'è un intervallo?**
- □ **Sì, c'è un intervallo di venti minuti.**

How much is a ticket?
How long is the concert without the interval?

Sports

6 Learning to ski
- ■ **Vorrei prendere lezioni di sci e noleggiare degli sci.**
- □ **Sì, allora le lezioni individuali costano 50.000 per un'ora e le lezioni di gruppo costano 25.000.**
- ■ **E gli sci?**
- □ **45.000 al giorno.**

Individual lessons plus skis cost:
95.000   85.000   75.000

Try it out

Odd man out

Find the word which doesn't belong.

| 1 | il biglietto | il canotto |
| | il botteghino | il programma |

| 2 | l'ombrellone | il lettino |
| | la sdraia | i pattini |

| 3 | il guardaroba | il golf |
| | la pallavolo | l'alpinismo |

| 4 | gli scarponi | i guanti |
| | il sandolino | gli sci |

| 5 | la barca a vela | la poltrona |
| | il posto in galleria | lo spettacolo |

Word search

There are 5 leisure spots hidden in the box. Can you find them?

T	U	A	B	T	C	D	E	M	G
A	I	L	M	O	N	P	Q	U	S
T	E	A	T	R	O	U	V	S	A
B	D	C	E	F	H	G	S	E	L
P	R	I	Q	M	O	S	N	O	S
V	U	N	Z	B	T	A	E	T	R
T	C	E	D	A	H	I	A	B	P
M	B	M	I	Z	N	D	F	G	H
D	I	A	R	P	I	L	Q	O	I
D	I	S	C	O	T	E	C	A	L

Holiday activities

Use the prompts to complete the questions/sentences.

1 swimming
2 things to see
3 hire an umbrella, deck-chair and sunbed
4 skiing lessons

1 Dove . . .?
2 Che cosa . . .?
3 Vorrei . . .
4 Vorrei . . .

Sound Check

With double consonants, the sound is prolonged:
ss, like 's' in 'bus stop'
    rosso   ros-so
nn, like 'n' in 'unnatural'
    anno   an-no

Practise on these words: **birra, cannelloni, frutta, gassato, panna, troppo**